T0354658

WE ALL ARE
CONNECTED

A Spiritual Approach toward
Our Personal Growth

K H A D I J E   B A Z Z I

WE ALL ARE CONNECTED
A SPIRITUAL APPROACH TOWARD OUR PERSONAL GROWTH

Scripture quotations taken from the Holy Bible, New International Version®, NIV® Copyright © 1973, 1978, 1984, 2011 by Biblica, Inc.® Used by permission. All rights reserved worldwide.

All Koranic scripture quotations are taken from the translation of Saheh International.

iUniverse books may be ordered through booksellers or by contacting:

iUniverse
1663 Liberty Drive
Bloomington, IN 47403
www.iuniverse.com
844-349-9409

Because of the dynamic nature of the internet, any web addresses or links contained in this book may have changed since publication and may no longer be valid. The views expressed in this work are solely those of the author and do not necessarily reflect the views of the publisher, and the publisher hereby disclaims any responsibility for them.

Any people depicted in stock imagery provided by Getty Images are models, and such images are being used for illustrative purposes only. Certain stock imagery © Getty Images.

ISBN: 978-1-6632-3007-2 (sc)
ISBN: 978-1-6632-3072-0 (hc)
ISBN: 978-1-6632-3008-9 (e)

Library of Congress Control Number: 2021921480

Print information available on the last page.

iUniverse rev. date: 11/16/2021

This book is dedicated to my lovely parents,
Haj Younes and Hajjah Sabah Bazzi.

We need more light about each other.
Light creates understanding,
Understanding creates love,
Love creates patience,
Patience creates unity
—Malcolm X

I am in love with every church
And mosque
And temple
And any kind of shrine
Because I know it is there
That people say the different names
Of the One God.
—Hafez

CONTENTS

Part III: We All Are Spiritually Connected

ACKNOWLEDGMENTS

First and foremost, I would like to thank the Almighty God for gifting me this opportunity to write this book. I could not do it without Him. God, I thank You for always blessing and protecting me. You have never left me alone. I am forever grateful to have You as the best planner for my life. I love You.

To my lovely parents, Haj Younes and Hajjah Sabah Bazzi: I cannot find the proper words to express the wisdom, encouragement, and love you have given me. I would not be the person I am today without your help and support. I would like to take this opportunity to thank you for all you have done for me. You are the greatest blessing in my life, and I am so grateful to have you as parents. I am so proud of you. I love you.

To my lovely siblings: Thanks for your unconditional support and love. You are always by my side when times are tough. I am so blessed to have you in my family. I love you.

I would like to thank all who helped and supported me in the process of writing this book. Thanks for believing in me. I heard each word and took it into consideration. Thanks for the positive feedback that encouraged me to keep writing and for the constructive criticism that taught me something new. It is comforting to know that I have such caring people surrounding me. A very special thanks to Professor Tallal Turfe, Imam Hassan Al-Qazwini, Imam Baqir Berry, and Judith LaForest. I am very grateful for the encouragement you have provided me.

Finally, I would like to thank you, my respected readers. I feel appreciative. I hope you enjoy reading this book and find it beneficial.

INTRODUCTION

We all are connected! Each one of us represents a spiritual being that has come and that will return to the same source at an appointed time. We all are swimming in one space and sharing the same earth and air. In this space, the sunlight does not distinguish white from black, rich from poor, man from woman, or CEO from janitor. It has been designed by God so we can all be together and share our mercy and compassion with one another.

Because we all are connected, I enjoy conversing with wise and spiritual people. I have been learning by opening my ears, mind, and heart to people of various religions and from various backgrounds. I find it really interesting how all of us are talking the same language—the language of humanity. All of us are looking for peace and happiness.

I had never thought to write a book, yet just recently, an inner voice whispered to me that I must do it. Because we all are connected, I decided to write this book for brothers and sisters in humanity. I want to share what I have learned from my own experiences and the experiences of others.

With the help of God and the scriptures from the Holy Koran (Saheeh International) and the Holy Bible (New International Version), I was able to write this book to help myself and readers to raise our level of spiritual awareness. In turn, this will help us reach our optimal well-being. This book is divided into three main parts. The first part highlights the spiritual connection with God. It explains how this holy connection can help us find the purpose of our essences in this life. It acknowledges how we can achieve inner peace and tranquility regardless of external circumstances. The second part contains numerous spiritual activities that will help increase our spiritual awareness and put us on the path toward our individual growth. The last part of this book emphasizes the importance of the human connection and how we can enhance our relationships to spread peace and love among us.

Although this book is not related to my studies and career field, I am very interested in self-development topics—particularly spiritual growth. I strongly believe that, as humans, we showed up here in this life for a purpose. Through the connection with the Almighty, we can understand ourselves and our real purpose, which in turn can put us on the right path, which brings inner peace, fulfillment, and satisfaction into our lives. I also believe that we all are students in this life regardless of our ages, titles, or statuses. Everything surrounding us, each challenge we face, each mistake we make, and each person we meet can be an opportunity for us to learn from.

Today I know that I am writing these words. But I do not know what tomorrow will hold for me or when it will be my time to return to the Creator. Before I leave, I want to ensure I spread my messages to whoever is meant to read this book. If you are reading these words now, I want you to know that there is a message waiting for you, and it is not a coincidence. My mission is that maybe one day someone somewhere will read this book and benefit from it, and that is enough for me.

God bless you!

PART I
Connection with God

The first part of this book addresses the most important connection in your life: your personal relationship with the Almighty God. After examining the following seven chapters, you will have a better understanding of who you really are and the purpose of your creation. This part also highlights the true meaning of happiness and how to achieve it. By reflecting on the following chapters, you will touch the presence of God in your daily life and learn how He is constantly taking care of you and listening to your prayers.

Who Are We and Why Are We Here?

God Is Our Perfect Designer

A Letter to God

Connection with God

Contentment: The Path to Real Happiness

Absolute Dependence on God

We Are Never Alone

Let Go and Let God

CHAPTER 1

Who Are We, and Why Are We Here?

The physical body is nothing but the house of the soul. Without the soul, the body is useless. A human being is a living soul with mind, emotion, and will. Through our souls, we can receive God's messages, feel the love of His words, and make the decision to connect with Him. On the other hand, the self, or the ego, is defined by our behaviors, traditions, beliefs, and personalities, which shape us directly through our environmental experiences.

How many times a day do you look in the mirror? What do you see? Do you find the same image every time? Easy questions, right? Now look at one of your old pictures, from when you were ten to fifteen years younger, and then immediately look in the mirror. Are you seeing the same image? Definitely not. There are a lot of differences between the two images. Did you ever ask yourself, "Where is that physical body that I occupied when I was ten to fifteen years younger?" It is known that the cells of human beings are constantly being regenerated. Hence, most of your physical body is always changing. So who are you? Which body defines you—the body in the picture from when you were ten to fifteen years younger, or the body you currently occupy? Indeed, the physical body that is constantly changing cannot define the essence of a person. There is another part inside of us that is boundless, has no form, and never dies. It is the soul that is breathed into the physical body, as the following scriptures illuminate:

> Then He proportioned him and breathed into him from
> His [created] soul and made for you hearing and vision
> and hearts; little are you grateful. (As-Sajdah 32:9)

> Then the Lord God formed a man from the dust of the ground and breathed into his nostrils the breath of life, and the man became a living being. (Genesis 2:7)

The physical body is temporary, while the soul is eternal. In fact, just when we begin to die, the soul will be taken out of the body and ascend to the Almighty God, as described in the following scriptures:

> Say, "The Angel of death will take you who has been entrusted with you. Then to your Lord you will be returned." (As-Sajdah 32:11)

> And the dust returns to the ground it came from, and the spirit returns to God who gave it. (Ecclesiastes 12:7)

Most of us are taking great care of our physical part by eating healthy food, drinking plenty of water, taking vitamins and minerals, and exercising. While this does not go unappreciated, our spiritual part is often ignored. Recalling that the body is temporary, and the soul is eternal, logically, do you not think that we should also take care of our souls? In fact, it is only when the soul is in harmony with its source that we can achieve inner peace, as we will discuss in far more detail in the coming chapters.

So what is the purpose of our existence? Why are we here? Let us look at the following scriptures that can help us find the answers:

> I did not create the jinn and mankind except to worship Me. (Adh-Dhariyat 51:56)

> Then did you think that We created you uselessly and that to Us you would not be returned? (Al-Mu'minun 23:115)

> Now all has been heard; here is the conclusion of the matter: Fear God and keep His commandments, for this is the duty of all mankind. (Ecclesiastes 12:13)

According to these scriptures, worshiping the Almighty God is our prime purpose in this life. In fact, the only reason why we were first created is to worship God. But here is the main question: are we truly worshiping God? To answer this question, we all need to understand what it means to worship God.

We spend most of our lives feeding our ego, the false self, which insists that we are separate from everyone, better than others, and always right. Our focus is on what we desire and what we want to attract into our lives. Deep down, many of us want to strive to be better than others. We want our spouses, children, jobs, paychecks, houses, physical appearances, running paces, cars, phones, and so on to be better than those of others. Even if we decide to do righteous deeds, such as building a religious institution or giving charity, we want our work to be acknowledged by others. The main problem with feeding the ego is that we can never feel satisfied and complete when we do so. Unfortunately, we take God out of the equation in most of our activities. Then we end up living in an illusion world called "ego illusion," which whispers to us, "We are great worshipers." Are we truly worshiping God? Nope, we are not! We must quit comparing ourselves to others. We must stop being greedy! We must let go of the belief that we are here to accumulate rewards or recognitions for our hard work. We have to pause for a moment and ask ourselves, "Where are we going? Are we living with a purpose?" Being aware of the quality of our thoughts, behaviors, and emotions will definitely help us refocus and realign our purpose in this life.

The soul that came from God will travel back to its source—the source of peace. To live on purpose is to allow our own souls to be in harmony with the source. To live on purpose is to prioritize God at any time and in any place. Undoubtedly, it is a challenging journey, and it requires a very high awareness of every single thought and action we perceive. To strengthen our relationship with God, we need to spend some quality time with Him by praying, reading, and reflecting on His scriptures and creations:

> O people of the Scripture, there has come to you Our Messenger making clear to you much of what you used to conceal of the Scripture and overlooking much. There

has come to you from Allah a light and a clear Book. By which Allah guides those who pursue His pleasure to the ways of peace and brings them out from darknesses into the light, by His permission, and guides them to a straight path. (Al-Ma'idah 5:15–16)

Indeed, in the creation of the heavens and the earth and the alternation of the night and the day are signs for those of understanding. (Al 'Imran 3:190)

Keep this Book of the Law always on your lips; meditate on it day and night, so that you may be careful to do everything written in it. Then you will be prosperous and successful. (Joshua 1:8)

When we prioritize our relationship with God, the source of being, we can cease demanding more of anything else. He will send us the right people at the proper time to help us. He will supply our needs to fulfill our destinies, and He will guide us to move forward in the righteous and straight path:

… And whoever holds firmly to Allah has [indeed] been guided to a straight path. (Al 'Imran 3:101)

In all your ways submit to Him, and He will make your paths straight. (Proverbs 3:6)

Indeed, all things were created for one ultimate purpose: to worship God. We all have the choice to shift our lives into meaningful lives of joy, purpose, and fulfillment. By keeping God first in our priorities, our lives will become more peaceful and secure. Through God we all are connected and responsible to help ourselves and others. Today let us be honest with ourselves and ask, "Are we truly living with a purpose?"

CHAPTER 2

God Is Our Perfect Designer

When God created us, He designed a specific purpose for each one of us. However, His ways in fulfilling His purposes are vastly different than ours, and sometimes we do not even understand them. To attain His objective, He can use any situation and anyone, even the evil ones.

Have you ever tried to put together a two-thousand-piece puzzle? While solving a jigsaw puzzle, we tend to take precautions to avoid losing any single piece, as we know that every piece counts. We often come across some pieces that do not look like they go together, but they do. We also come across other pieces that look like they go together, but they do not. Solving a puzzle is a journey of a person who decides to put it together piece by piece to complete the big picture. During this journey, the person must trust the designer of that puzzle to not have left out any pieces, and that every single piece will be used to complete the whole picture. That is exactly how life turns out. Each one of us has a unique journey and a purpose to accomplish. Sometimes things look great and we feel satisfied. There are also times when we face challenges and turbulences. In these moments, things look blurred and confusing, and we often feel frustrated, scared, and angry. In fact, everything we face in this life represents a single piece of a puzzle. This puzzle is the journey of our lives. When we connect all the events that seemed unrelated to us in the past, we begin to see a clear picture of our journey. The good news here is that our journey has a designer—a perfect designer: the Almighty God.

> Indeed, all things We created with predestination. (Al Qamar 54:49)

> Say, "Never will we be struck except by what Allah has decreed for us; He is our protector." And upon Allah let the believers rely. (At-Tawbah 9:51)

> And we know that in all things God works for the good of those who love him, who have been called according to his purpose. (Romans 8:28)

> Many are the plans in a person's heart, but it is the Lord's purpose that prevails. (Proverbs 19:21)

In His Holy Books, God illustrates the best stories to teach us how He can fit together every aspect in our own lives, even the things that make no sense for us, for our own good. The story of Joseph ("Yusuf" in Arabic) is a great example of this point.

> We relate to you, [O Muhammad], the best of stories in what We have revealed to you of this Qur'an although you were, before it, among the unaware. (Yusuf 12:3)

> Certainly were there in Joseph and his brothers signs for those who ask. (Yusuf 12:7)

In brief, Joseph was the favorite son among the twelve sons of the prophet Jacob. Joseph's brothers were jealous of him. They plotted to kill him, but one of the brothers argued against killing him and suggested they throw Joseph into a well instead of killing him. After throwing Joseph in to a well, they brought back Joseph's shirt, covered with false blood, to inform their father that Joseph was dead.

> They said, "O our father, indeed we went racing each other and left Joseph with our possessions, and a wolf ate him ..." And they brought upon his shirt false blood. [Jacob] said, "Rather, your souls have enticed you

something, so patience is most fitting. And Allah is the one sought for help against that which you describe." (Yusuf 12:17–18)

Then they got Joseph's robe, slaughtered a goat and dipped the robe in the blood. They took the ornate robe back to their father and said, "We found this. Examine it to see whether it is your son's robe." (Genesis 37:31–32)

Then a passing caravan stopped by the well and saw Joseph inside. They retrieved him and sold him into slavery in Egypt, to a very wealthy man called Potiphar (known as "Al-Aziz" in Islam). Years later, Joseph was wrongly accused by the wife of Potiphar, so he ended up in jail for many years for a crime he did not commit.

… She said, "What is the recompense of one who intended evil for your wife but that he be imprisoned or a painful punishment?" (Yusuf 12:25)

When his master heard the story his wife told him, saying, "This is how your slave treated me", he burned with anger. Joseph's master took him and put him in prison, the place where the king's prisoners were confined. (Genesis 39:19–20)

Later on, the king was informed that Joseph was gifted with the ability to interpret dreams. So when Joseph interpreted the king's dream, the king promoted Joseph from a slave and prisoner to a position of power to help prepare Egypt for the future from the severe famine.

And the king said, "Bring him to me; I will appoint him exclusively for myself." And when he spoke to him, he said, "Indeed, you are today established [in position] and trusted." (Yusuf 12:54)

Then Pharaoh said to Joseph, "Since God has made all this known to you, there is no one so discerning and wise as you. You shall be in charge of my palace, and all my people are to submit to your orders. Only with respect to the throne will I be greater than you." (Genesis 41:39–41)

Years later, when the famine affected his family in Canaan, Joseph's brothers arrived in Egypt to get food. Joseph recognized his brothers, but they did not recognize him. Eventually he revealed himself to his brothers and forgave them of all the evils done against him, and he was able to arrange the entire family's relocation to Egypt.

He said, "No blame will there be upon you today. Allah will forgive you; and He is the most merciful of the merciful." (Yusuf 12:92)

And now, do not be distressed and do not be angry with yourselves for selling me here, because it was to save lives that God sent me ahead of you … So then, it was not you who sent me here, but God … (Genesis 45:5, 8)

You intended to harm me, but God intended it for good to accomplish what is now being done, the saving of many lives. (Genesis 50:20)

After all Joseph went through because of his brothers' evil acts, he forgave them. He was looking wisely at the big picture, and he trusted his God, who allowed him to go through all these hardships to save many lives.

Being sold into slavery, being accused by the wife of Potiphar, and being unjustly thrown in jail were definitely not pleasant occurrences for Joseph. Nevertheless, God used all these struggles for good. Only God could let the king see a dream that caused him to seek out a dream interpreter who would eventually release Joseph from jail. Only God could promote Joseph from an enslaved prisoner to a ruler in Egypt. Only God could allow the famine to take place at that specific time so that Joseph's family in Canaan would be affected. Only God could reunite Joseph with his father and family. Only God could connect all these events to fulfill Joseph's destiny. What a great planner our God is!

… But they plan, And Allah plans. And Allah is the best of planners. (Al Anfal 8:30)

"For I know the plans I have for you," declares the Lord, "plans to prosper you and not to harm you, plans to give you hope and a future." (Jeremiah 29:11)

Today you may be facing some challenges at home, work, or some other areas in your life. Who knows, perhaps someone has made false accusations about you and you have ended up suffering alone. Whatever challenges you are facing today, remember Joseph's journey and how God used every single challenge to yield something good.

Always remember that your journey has a perfect designer and that He is going to use every obstacle for your own development.

CHAPTER 3

Contentment: The Key to Real Happiness

In this life, there are plenty of things that can bring us pleasure. These things could be related to wealth, status, relationships, fame, or possessions. However, have we ever asked ourselves whether these pleasant moments are permanent or not? Why does the same child who was so excited about a new toy that was handed to him later become bored and want something else? Why does the same couple who were so eager to have a baby in the beginning of their marriage later, after having many kids, get busy with life and find that they are no longer as excited as they once were?

Many people believe that amassing large sums of money can bring them happiness, but they end up psychologically depressed and anxious as a result of having a fear of losing their money. Does the number in our checking account represent the key to our happiness? What about the names of the universities we graduated from, the cars we drive, the brand names of our clothes and shoes, the number of friends we have, or the number of awards and certificates we achieve? In fact, none of these can define our real happiness, because they are all material things. Surely, we want it and enjoy such things. They bring us some pleasure. Nevertheless, these worldly pleasures are temporary. The enjoyment will vanish immediately upon the completion of what we desire. Unfortunately, we get too attached to it, and we ignore the fact that most of these materials things were sent from God to us as gifts so we can use them to accomplish our purpose in this life. Yet we focus on these gifts, and we forget the giver and the purpose of this life.

Know that the life of this world is but amusement and diversion and adornment and boasting to one another and competition in increase of wealth and children … And what is the worldly life except the enjoyment of delusion. (Al Hadid 57:20)

Beautified for people is the love of that which they desire—of women and sons, heaped-up sums of gold and silver, fine branded horses, and cattle and tilled land. That is the enjoyment of worldly life, but Allah has with Him the best return. (Al 'Imran 3:14)

For the love of money is a root of all kinds of evil. Some people, eager for money, have wandered from the faith and pierced themselves with many griefs. (1 Timothy 6:10)

These scriptures illustrate different forms of pleasures that human beings are constantly seeking in this worldly life. These material pleasures derived from material goods are nothing but illusion. In fact, the more we accumulate things we truly do not need, the more we feel that we need more. It is a craving that can never be satisfied, and it will lead us to sign up for a life full of dissatisfaction as seeking more of everything becomes our jailer. Being aware of this reality will absolutely help us refocus on our purposes in this life.

If material things are not indicative of true happiness, then what is real happiness? How can we be happy regardless of socioeconomic status? The answer to these questions is linked to our connection with the Almighty God. While worldly pleasures are expressed in the world of form, the connection with God can transcend the physical world. True happiness is the ability to feel the presence of God in anywhere and at all times. True happiness is the inner peace that can be achieved only by the remembrance of God in all aspects of our lives. The key to real happiness is to be satisfied and grateful with your current situation regardless of external circumstances. To be content is to believe that there is a time for everything and a season for every activity according to God's plan. The following scriptures highlight the relationship between the contentment and the spiritual connection with God:

> Those who have believed and whose hearts are assured by the remembrance of Allah. Unquestionably, by the remembrance of Allah hearts are assured. (Ar-Ra'd 13:28)

> And whoever turns away from My remembrance—indeed, he will have a depressed life, and We will gather him on the Day of Resurrection blind. (Taha 20:124)

> You make known to me the path of life; you will fill me with joy in your presence, with eternal pleasures at your right hand. (Psalm 16:11)

> I am not saying this because I am in need, for I have learned to be content whatever the circumstances. I know what it is to be in need, and I know what it is to have plenty. I have learned the secret of being content in any and every situation, whether well fed or hungry, whether living in plenty or in want. (Philippians 4:11–12)

To build a spiritual connection with the Almighty God, we must seek to know God. Believing in Him is important, but it is not enough. We must have a conscious contact with our Higher Power. The first step we must take is to educate ourselves and then our children about the Creator of the universe. God definitely wants us to sincerely worship Him, follow His instructions, and do virtuous deeds to reward us in the hereafter. Nonetheless, God also wants each one of us to have a good life here as well. When we follow the instructions of the Lord and pursue righteousness, God will provide us good lives full of joy, peace, and hope:

> Whoever does righteousness, whether male or female, while he is a believer—We will surely cause him to live a good life, and We will surely give them their reward [in the Hereafter] according to the best of what they used to do. (An-Nahl 16:97)

Blessed are those whose ways are blameless, who walk according to the law of the Lord. Blessed are those who keep his statutes and seek him with all their heart—they do no wrong but follow his ways. (Psalm 119:1–3)

This is the path to real happiness. This is the spiritual connection that blows away all kinds of anxieties and worries. This is the only connection that does not depend on wealth, fame, age, gender, race, or status. It is the holy connection that is mainly built on faith and trust in Him. This is the connection that takes us to a different world free from any material things. It is the world of the purest love that can fill the voids in our hearts, which in turn can ultimately bring meaning and great satisfaction to our existence. The love of God is absolute love; once we taste it, we will never look for any replacement in place of Him. Our Lord is unlike anything or anyone we could ever imagine. Indeed, He is the real Lover!

Let us end this chapter by meditating on the following elegant words from the "Whispered Prayer of The Lovers" by Imam Al-Sajjad (peace be upon him), the great-grandson of the Prophet Muhammad (peace be upon him). Let us read it with our whole hearts and let us learn what it means to have an intimate connection with God that leads to a contented life. This beautiful prayer is meant to be read by any believer on this planet. While reading, allow your spirit to fly to the world of the purest love and affection.

THE WHISPERED PRAYER OF THE LOVERS

In the Name of ALLAH, the All-compassionate
the All-merciful, the All-compassionate

O! My God, who is the one to have tasted the sweetness of your
love and then looked for a replacement in place of you?
Who can claim to have become familiar with your
nearness, then wanted removal from you?
O My God, include us among the ones whom you
have chosen for your nearness and friendship,

And (include us among the ones) whom you have
purified through your love and affection,
And (Include us among the ones) whom you
have given the desire for with you,
And (include us among the ones) who are pleased with all your decisions,

.

.

.

I ask you for your love, and also love for those who love you,
And I ask you to make me love every deed which
will bring me to your proximity,
And that you make yourself more beloved to
me than anything other than you
and make my love for you to lead me to pleasing you
And make my longing for you to protect me against disobeying you!
honor me by allowing me to gaze upon you,
While you are gazing upon me with affection and tenderness,
And do not turn your face away from me,
and make me one with whom you are happy with
and that am in your favored position!
O Responder, O Most Merciful of the merciful!

From "Whispered Prayer of the Lovers" by Imam Al-
Sajjad (peace be upon him), the great-grandson of the
Prophet Muhammad (peace be upon him).

CHAPTER 4

We Are Never Alone

W e all face those dark days when we feel that we need to talk to someone to share our problems and get some advice. During those times, many of us think of contacting a close friend or a family member. Before contacting that person, we often make sure that the time is convenient, and then we check whether that person is willing to talk. Sometimes we end up not talking to that person and become frustrated and anxious. What should we do in that time? What if we were able to talk to that person but did not receive the anticipated support? What if someone has no one to turn to? Whatever it is that makes us feel lonely, we must know that we are never alone! The Creator of the entire universe is always with us. In fact, He is always available, and He never sleeps. Better yet, we do not need Wi-Fi or a cell phone to talk to Him. He is closer to us than our jugular veins:

> … He is with you wherever you are … (Al-Hadid 57:4)

> …We are closer to him than [his] jugular vein. (Qaf 50:16)

> … for the Lord your God will be with you wherever you go. (Joshua 1:9)

> "Am I only a God nearby," declares the Lord, "and not a God far away?" (Jeremiah 23:23)

Talking to God through prayer is a great approach to strengthen our bond with Him and share all our needs and desires with Him without worrying about the convenience of time or place, By nature, human beings are so vulnerable, and we all need His help, strength, and mercy.

> And Allah wants to lighten for you [your difficulties]; and mankind was created weak. (Al-Nisa 4:28)

> So do not fear, for I am with you; do not be dismayed, for I am your God. I will strengthen you and help you; I will uphold you with my righteous right hand. (Isaiah 41:10)

Whether you are a Christian, a Muslim, or any human being who believes in God, you need to spend some quality time with God. We may differ on the ways of how we are approaching God in prayer. For instance, while Muslims must pray a certain number of times per day, Christians do not need to do so. Whether you use prayer books or prewritten prayers, or you just sincerely speak to God from your heart, prayer is a time of personal communion with God. The more we pray, the more we will feel His presence in our lives.

In the same way the physical body needs oxygen to survive, our spiritual well-being needs its spiritual oxygen to survive as well. While none of us can see the oxygen with the naked eye, everyone agrees that we cannot live without it. Similarly, if we disconnect from our Almighty God, we will lose our inner peace, and we will end up feeling sad and crushed. "And whoever turns away from My remembrance—indeed, he will have a depressed life, and We will gather him on the Day of Resurrection blind" (Taha 20:124). By consistently reading His scriptures and reciting prayers (or supplications), we will build a solid connection with God and experience His presence on a daily basis. Through prayer we can show God that we have hope, belief, trust, and faith in Him. Through prayer we can acknowledge our weaknesses and reinforce our needs to Him. Genuinely, prayer is the spiritual nutrition for the soul. It is one of the greatest blessings we can access anytime and anywhere. It is available to everyone, and we should all be grateful for that gift.

There is a powerful supplication, "Dua Al Jawshan Al Kabeer," which has been narrated from the Prophet Muhammad (peace be upon him), who received it from the angel Gabriel during a battle. It is a powerful supplication that leads the reader to know God through His names and attributes. It shows how lovely, merciful, and gracious our Almighty God is. This supplication contains one hundred sections, and it contains only one request: "Praise be to You, there is no God but You, Help us, Help us, Protect us from the Fire, O Lord." The remaining is all about calling God's names and attributes. Let us read the following two selected sections from this supplication:

(Section # 11)
O Provider in my hardship,
O Source of Hope in my misfortune,
O Companion in my isolation,
O Fellow Traveler in my journey,
O Friend in my ease,
O Rescuer from my trials,
O Guide in my errancy,
O Resource in my neediness,
O Shelter in my helplessness,
O Deliverer from my fears.
Praise be to You, there is no God but You, Help us,
Help us, Protect us from the Fire, O Lord

(Section # 59)
O Friend of he who has no friend,
O Physician of he who has no physician,
O Responder to he who has no responder,
O Affectionate One to he whom none holds in affection,
O Friend of he who has no friend,
O Helper of he who has no help,
O Guide of he who has no guide,
O Associate of the forlorn,
O Merciful One towards he on whom no one has mercy,
O Companion of he who has no companion.

> Praise be to You, there is no God but You, Help us,
> Help us, Protect us from the Fire, O Lord

By ruminating on these two sections, we feel that we are never alone. By reciting the full supplication and reflecting on it, we can educate ourselves and our children about God. It is important to mention here that this supplication is known to be read during the holy month of Ramadan, but we do not have to wait till then to read it. Also, this supplication is not meant to be read by Muslims only. It is recommended to everyone who believes in God, regardless of his or her culture, traditions, or religion.

This earthly life is temporary, and it is not designed to be perfect for anyone. We all are struggling in different ways. Many of us do not have friends or partners. Some of us are living alone, away from our families. Many among us have many people in our lives, and yet we still feel lonely. Some of us are dealing with health issues and the medical reports are not promising. Many of us are facing unfair situations. Whatever we are facing that makes us feel alone or lonely, we should constantly remind ourselves that we are never alone. God is closer to us than we think. Today, the Creator of the entire universe is sending a special message to you. He is reminding you about His words to comfort you:

> And be patient for the decision of your Lord, for indeed,
> you are in Our eyes… (At-Tur 52:48)

> I will instruct you and teach you in the way you should
> go; I will counsel you with My loving eye on you. (Psalm
> 32:8)

CHAPTER 5

Let Go and Let God

During the good times, we all tend to be satisfied and happy with our lives. However, when we face difficulties and challenges, we often get depressed and doubtful, and we blame each other for our problems. Sometimes we unconsciously blame God for allowing bad things to happen to us. What should we do when facing adversity to avoid losing hope? To prevent despair, the only safe path we can follow is to let go and let God handle the situation. Amid the difficulties, we must have confidence that there exists a divine Creator who will work out all things for our good, no matter what the circumstances are. Letting go simply means turning to God and submitting to His will.

> And will provide for him where he does not expect. And whoever relies upon Allah—Then He is sufficient for him. Indeed, Allah will accomplish His purpose. Allah has already set for everything a [decreed] extent. (At-Talaq 65:3)

> Trust in the Lord with all your heart and lean not on your own understanding; in all your ways submit to him, and he will make your paths straight. (Proverbs 3:5–6)

Diamonds are crystals of pure carbon that have formed under conditions of intense heat and pressure, and that is what causes the carbon to crystalize over time. Without that high intensity and pressure, diamonds can never be strong and beautiful. The same principle applies to human beings. It is the pressure and the challenges that we face in our lives that make us grow. Can we start looking at our challenges from this perspective? From now on, let us pause and reflect on every single challenge we are facing. And instead of being bitter or complaining about the situation, let us trust God's plan and ask ourselves, "How can I grow? What lesson(s) can I learn?" Let us be just like diamonds: strong and beautiful. Let us trust God—the God who comforts His true believers by saying,

> So do not weaken and do not grieve, and you will be superior if you are [true] believers. (Al 'Imran 3:139)

> Consider it pure joy, my brothers, and sisters, whenever you face trials of many kinds, because you know that the testing of your faith produces perseverance. Let perseverance finish its work so that you may be mature and complete, not lacking anything. (James 1:2–4)

Moses's mother was selected by God to be an example of the women of faith, who are mentioned in the holy books. She took a major leap of faith and placed her baby in the Nile River. This Jewish mother is an ordinary human being, just as all of us are. However, she was very special in her faith and her strong belief in her God's will. After Pharaoh had ordered all the newborn babies to be killed, the mother of Moses decided to turn to God and trust His providential care to take care of her and her baby.

> And We inspired to the mother of Moses, "Suckle him; but when you fear for him, cast him into the river and do not fear and do not grieve. Indeed We will return him to you and will make him [one] of the messengers." (Al-Qasas 28:7)

> But when she could hide him no longer, she got a papyrus basket for him and coated it with tar and pitch. Then she placed the child in it and put it among the reeds along the bank of the Nile. (Exodus 2:3)

When Moses's mother placed her baby in the Nile River, she had no idea that her child would grow up to be one of God's greatest messengers. She had a firm hope and faith in God's grand plan. Moses was chosen by God to rescue the Jewish people from slavery in Egypt. So He ordained the baby to refuse to accept all the wet nurses in the palace. Out of His mercy, God fulfilled His promise to this mother who put her trust in Him.

> And We had prevented from him [all] wet nurses before, so she said, "Shall I direct you to a household that will be responsible for him for you while they are to him [for his upbringing] sincere?" So We restored him to his mother that she might be content and not grieve and that she would know that the promise of Allah is true. But most of them [i.e., the people] do not know. (Al-Qasas 28:12–13)

> …So the girl went and got the baby's mother. Pharaoh's daughter said to her, "Take this baby and nurse him for me, and I will pay you." So the woman took the baby and nursed him. (Exodus 2:8–9)

What a great planner our God is! As a reward of her faith, God not only allowed her to raise her own child through his nursing years but also allowed her to be paid to nurse him. Because of her unshakeable faith, God was using this woman as an instrument to achieve His purposes in the life of Moses and the nation of Israel. Let us learn from this woman how to trust God during times of adversity.

We all face adversities from time to time, and we sometimes do not understand what God is doing. "As you do not know the path of the wind, or how the body is formed in a mother's womb, so you cannot understand the work of God, the Maker of all things" (Ecclesiastes 11:5). For instance, sometimes a close friend hurts you, and the friendship suddenly ends. God knows that this friendship is not a nourishing or an empowering relationship for you. So out of His mercy He ends it for your benefit, even if you do not see it while you are still grieving. Therefore we must always remember that when God takes something away from us, He is genuinely protecting us from something worse that could happen to us.

Likewise, sometimes we hate to face some challenges because they make us feel uncomfortable although they will be good for us. While growth can be painful for us, we should always keep in mind that suffering produces perseverance and that our characters will be developed through the hardships. That is exactly what God describes in His words:

> ... But perhaps you hate a thing and it is good for you; and perhaps you love a thing and it is bad for you. And Allah Knows, while you know not. (Al-Baqarah 2:216)

> And we know that in all things God works for the good of those who love him, who have been called according to his purpose. (Romans 8:28)

> Not only so, but we also glory in our sufferings, because we know that suffering produces perseverance; perseverance, character; and character, hope. (Romans 5:3–4)

There are some areas in our lives where we need to stop chasing and demanding, instead starting to trust God. Maybe it is an unhealthy relationship, seeking approval from others, or the absurd idea that we cannot be happy because we are missing people or things in our lives. Whatever that false attachment is, it is time to let go and trust God. Who knows, maybe if we let it go, God will restore it to us in a better way as He did this with Moses's mother. Or maybe He will put in our path exceptional people with whom we form friendships that exceed our expectations. "... If Allah knows [any] good in your hearts, He will give you [something] better than what was taken from you ..." (Al-Anfal 8:70).

By letting go and letting God, we acknowledge the presence of God and allow Him to do work in our lives. Today, let us ask God to use us as an instrument to fulfill His purposes on Earth as He did with Moses's mother. Who knows, maybe one act of faith from one of us, with a pure intention, can have a huge impact on different generations. So let go and let God!

CHAPTER 6

Absolute Dependence on God

When we were kids, we were taught to study and work hard in school to get good grades so we could graduate, find good jobs, make families, and settle down in our lives. During this journey, we have learned how to be self-reliant. In fact, we did a great job at convincing ourselves that we can receive whatever we desire by relying on our own abilities. Then we developed a belief that we, ourselves, are the ones who control our own lives. So we unconsciously developed an attachment to material things, people, and even our own skills. Things suddenly happen, and we start losing things such as health, possessions, money, jobs, or maybe people, such as close friends or family members. Then we face extremely traumatic experiences, which lead some of us to despair and depression. The mistake we make here is that we forget that in this life everything is temporary and nothing will last forever. However, if we rely only on our Creator, He will never put us down.

Having good friends, coworkers, and even family members is indeed a blessing from God to each one of us, and we should always be grateful for that. It is a wonderful feeling to have people in our lives who support us and make us feel good all the time. However, if we rely on these people as our only source of support or approval, then we will often get discouraged and disappointed because people are limited with what they can offer to others. Plus, they are not always available for us, including the ones with the pure intention. Unfortunately, even the closest people to us can sometimes turn on us and fail us. Right now, we are probably fully dependent on some people in our lives, and we are not aware of that. It is not even fair to them. Our happiness is not their accountability. They already have their own problems. God, however, is near to us and hears the voice of each one of us. He can fulfill all our needs and wishes. He can meet all our expectations, as described in the following scriptures:

> … And whoever relies upon Allah—then He is sufficient for him. Indeed, Allah will accomplish His purpose … (At-Talaq 65:3)

> … Rely upon Allah. Indeed, Allah loves those who rely [upon Him]—If Allah should aid you, no one can overcome you; but if He should forsake you, who is there that can aid you after Him? And upon Allah let the believers rely [upon Him]. (Al 'Imran 3:159–160)

> The Lord is good to those whose hope is in Him, to the one who seeks Him. (Lamentations 3:25)

> It is better to take refuge in the Lord than to trust in humans. (Psalm 118:8).

The prophet Moses (peace be upon him), who was selected by God as a religious leader, is a great example of a spiritual being who teaches us how to have an absolute dependence on God when harsh adversities befall us. When he stood in front of the Red Sea, Pharaoh's army was approaching from behind, and the mountains surrounded them. Although some of Moses's companions felt very doubtful and overtaken, the prophet Moses felt strong and courageous.

> And when the two companies saw one another, the companions of Moses said, "Indeed, we are to be overtaken!" [Moses] said, "No! Indeed, with me is my Lord; He will guide me." Then We inspired to Moses, "Strike with your staff the sea", and it parted, and each portion was like a great towering mountain. (Ash-Shu'ara 26:61–63)

24

> Then Moses stretched out his hand over the sea, and all that night the Lord drove the sea back with a strong east wind and turned it into dry land. The waters were divided. (Exodus 14:21)

What a strong faith the prophet Moses had! As a reward for that unshakeable faith, the Creator of the universe parted the Red Sea so Moses and his followers could cross it and make their way to the other end. This is not just a story to entertain us and our kids. It is an eternal lesson to mankind. It teaches us that there is always hope in God and that there is nothing impossible for Him. The same God who turned the sea into dry land for Moses can turn our difficulties into ease and our sorrow into joy.

All of us are facing challenges and difficulties. It may seem impossible and out of our control. Without Him, we are nothing, we can accomplish nothing, and we will feel desperate and detached. Yet if we truly depend on God and not on ourselves or our resources, we will have the opportunity to experience His power, promises, and provision. Indeed, an absolute dependence on God is our safest path for success in this life and in the hereafter.

CHAPTER 7

A Letter to God

Then the Lord replied:
Write down the revelation
and make it plain on tablets
so that a herald may run with it.
For the revelation awaits an appointed time;
it speaks of the end
and will not prove false.
Though it linger, wait for it;
it will certainly come
and will not delay.
—Habakkuk 2:2–3

We all have goals and dreams we would like to achieve in our lifetimes. Many of us tend to share these dreams with friends or family members, as we think that these people can play decent roles in supporting and helping us. That is true; however, we cannot expect them to see and understand our visions. Let us be honest with ourselves. How many times have we shared our goals and dreams with some friends or family members, and instead of encouraging us to pursue them, they shot us down because they thought it was not possible? Well, they were right; it was not possible for them, because they could not visualize our dreams. Our goals and dreams are uniquely designed for us and not for others.

Maybe you feel discouraged or scared to dream again because you let someone's opinion become your reality. Yet there is a voice inside you that whispers all day long, telling you that you have something special and that there is a greatness and power inside of you. Well, have you ever thought to write a letter to God—a letter in which you can share all your thoughts, emotions, and feelings with Him?

Writing a letter to God is one of the most effective and creative ways to communicate with God. It is a way for us to surrender all our problems to Him, and a technique for us to share all our dreams and goals with Him. By physically writing the words down and addressing the letter straight to God, we open ourselves up to His guidance. Now, would you like to write a letter to God? Let us get started.

Find a quiet room and make sure you are in an environment where you can be alone with your thoughts and will not be interrupted during the process. Grab a notebook and a pen. Start your letter by thanking God for all the gifts and the talents you already have in your life. Ask Him to not take it away and to add blessing to it. Then write down all your needs and desires. Be open and honest with God. Share with Him all your thoughts, feelings, and worries. Most importantly, do not be shy! Tell him what you would like to invite into your life. Share with Him your wishes and dreams, and never think that is too much. Why? Because there is nothing impossible with God. While you are writing, remind yourself that you are writing to the one who creates and rules the entire universe. If you still feel you are asking too much, pause for a moment and remind yourself about His words and promises:

> And when My servants ask you, [O Muhammad], concerning Me—indeed I am near. I respond to the invocation of the supplicant when he calls upon Me. So, let them respond to Me [by obedience] and believe in Me that they may be [rightly] guided. (Al Baqara 2:186)

> And your Lord says, "Call upon Me; I will respond to you." Indeed, those who disdain My worship will enter Hell [rendered] contemptible. (Ghafir 40:60)

> His command is only when He intends a thing that He says to it, "Be," and it is. (Ya-Sin 36:82)

> Ask and it will be given to you; seek and you will find; knock and the door will be opened to you. For everyone who asks receives; the one who seeks finds; and to the one who knocks, the door will be opened. (Matthew 7:7–8)

> Call to me and I will answer you and tell you great and unsearchable things you do not know. (Jeremiah 33:3).

> I am the Lord, the God of all mankind. Is anything too hard for me? (Jeremiah 32:27).

Make sure to prepare your letter, which contains the list of all your needs, and keep it in a private place. Every once in a while, take that letter and read it with faith. After one year, go over the same list. You will be astonished at how many of your prayers were already answered.

How many times in the past have we asked God to deliver us from troubles and to take away the problems we face? Did He not answer most of it? Yes, He did save us from most of our problems. In fact, lots of our prayers were answered, but we tend to forget. Writing a letter to God is a way to remind ourselves about the prayers that we might forget in future.

Because we, human beings, are finite and limited in our knowledge and wisdom, we often ask God for things that could be harmful for us. The following scriptures offer some answers as to why we sometimes ask and do not receive the answers:

> And man supplicates for evil [when angry] as he supplicates for good, and man is ever hasty. (Al-Isra 17:11)

> When you ask, you do not receive, because you ask with wrong motives, that you may spend what you get on your pleasures. (James 4:3)

Thus, because of the mercy of God, some of our prayers will not be answered immediately. We must have faith and trust in Him. He sees the bigger picture of our lives, and He knows what is best for us. In fact, when we do not receive an answer immediately, He will always reward us for our prayers in different ways. He might save us from some tragedies that would have befallen us. Or maybe He will save the reward of our prayers for the hereafter.

Writing a letter to God is one of the greatest methods to communicate with Him. In addition to sharing our needs with God, this approach nourishes our souls and strengthens the bonds between our souls and the Lord. Today let each one of us decide to write a letter to God. We do not have to share these letters with anyone. Let us take it as an attempt to establish a new relationship with the Almighty. Later, after seeing the positive results of this method in your own life, help someone else. Encourage your friends, your family members, and all your loved ones to write their own letters to the Creator of the universe. Let us spread the kindness all together!

PART II

Let Us Grow Together

This part presents several spiritual activities that help us change our perception and the way we see the world around us. Here I selected eleven topics that can help us increase our awareness, develop a balanced lifestyle, and make us a better version of ourselves. At the end of each chapter, take a moment to pause and reflect on your life, behavior, and belief.

CHAPTER 8

The Power of Forgiveness

Being hurt by a person we trusted is one of the worst feelings. This chapter addresses the topic of suffering from a broken heart and the power of forgiveness to heal it.

It was just yesterday that we were enjoying time with our loved ones. It was yesterday when we felt secure, blessed, and happy simply by being with our loved ones. Suddenly we woke up to find that it was only a dream. We opened our eyes wider to see where they went to. We recognize faces and bodies, but their souls are no longer familiar, as they sit and mind their own business. We are left alone with broken hearts. Often we find ourselves waiting for them to rekindle the joy they previously filled us with. We pray, cry, and grieve, but their old selves are never restored. This is the journey of a broken heart that many of us are left to face. Whether the person who is no longer familiar is a family member, close friend, or spouse, we cannot deny the emotional upheaval that we have experienced. Today we are going to make an important modification in ourselves. We will allow the peace and love back into our lives. But this time we are not waiting for anyone. Today we are born again to be happy and to live a life of purpose. Today we want to forgive ourselves first, and then those who caused our heartbreak.

Many of us experience the feeling of being heartbroken when someone lets us down. Whether it is a physical or emotional letdown, it is a painful experience that we must acknowledge and learn from. Once we are able to do so, we will be able to move forward. As human beings, it is very common to feel the need to take revenge on those who wronged us. During these moments of resentment, we fail to realize that by holding a grudge against others we only delay our personal growth. There is a powerful saying by Nelson Mandela that goes, "Resentment is like drinking poison and hoping it will kill your enemies." By constantly living in the past and replaying the story of how someone wronged us, we only block the path to moving forward. It is time now to end that chapter and live in the present.

By focusing on the past, we are missing the present moments that could hold many new opportunities that we have been waiting for. Maybe you are a single woman or man and you are looking for a partner in your life. By focusing on your previous failed relationships, you might miss lots of opportunities to meet new people and the right partner. Do yourself a favor and stop wasting your time and energy on people or things from the past, which is no longer within your control. The best action we can take is to let the past go and forgive others, but we must never forget the lessons learned.

How are we to let go of the negative feelings? Do we really have to suppress these emotions to move forward in our lives? Suppressing emotions can lead to serious health problems. Hence, we must acknowledge that it is okay to validate our feelings and even cry. Crying is a healthy way to express emotions. In fact, crying can benefit both the mind and body; it is one of the greatest ways to remove chemicals and hormones that build up during emotional stress. Being honest with ourselves in expressing our emotions will indeed help us move forward through life. The next step is to decide to forgive all the people who have hurt us. We must always remember that forgiveness is not about absolving others at all; it is only about our inner peace. In fact, we can never achieve the spirit of tranquility in our hearts if we keep engaging with anger and resentful thoughts toward anyone we believe has wronged us.

When we turn our pain and suffering over to God, He will guide us in moving on and moving forward. Through God we will be able to slowly bring peace back into our lives. In fact, only God can remove the bitterness from our hearts and replace it with joy. The Arabic name "Al-Jabbar" is one of the ninety-nine names of God in Islam, and it has multiple meanings. One of the meanings of that name is "the one who mends what is broken." Our Creator is close to the brokenhearted, and He is the only one who can mend our broken hearts. Hence, every time we feel broken, we should look to the one who has the attribute of mending the heartbroken.

> And when My servants ask you, [O Muhammad], concerning Me—indeed I am near. I respond to the invocation of the supplicant when he calls upon Me. So, let them respond to Me [by obedience] and believe in Me that they may be [rightly] guided. (Al-Baqarah 2:186)

> The Lord is close to the brokenhearted and saves those who are crushed in spirit. (Psalm 34:18)

Whether it is intentional or unintentional, we all make mistakes and mistreat one another. God wants us to forgive each other no matter how many times people hurt us. "So watch yourselves. 'If your brother or sister sins against you, rebuke them; and if they repent, forgive them. Even if they sin against you seven times in a day and seven times come back to you saying, 'I repent,' you must forgive them'" (Luke 17:3–4).

The first and the most important person you must forgive is yourself. We all have done things we are not proud of. By blaming ourselves and constantly feeling guilty, we are unconsciously punishing ourselves. Embracing the concept of self-compassion in this matter will definitely lead us to forgive ourselves from any mistake and stop dwelling on the past. Knowing that our merciful God forgives all sins, and that the door of the repentance is always open, will help us not give up on ourselves.

> Say, "O My servants who have transgressed against themselves [by sinning], do not despair of the mercy of Allah. Indeed, Allah forgives all sins. Indeed, it is He who is the Forgiving, the Merciful." (Al Zumar 39:53)

> Forget the former things; do not dwell on the past. (Isaiah 43:18)

> The Lord our God is merciful and forgiving, even though we have rebelled against him. (Daniel 9:9)

By practicing forgiveness, we have an opportunity to grow spiritually even when we feel mistreated or abused. For instance, forgiving others can make us healthier, more steadfast, and less vulnerable to the people who have caused us grief. "And whoever is patient and forgives—indeed, that is of the matters [requiring] determination" (Ash-Shura 42:43).

Forgiving others is an act of mercy and compassion toward ourselves. By embracing forgiveness, we can embrace a healthy life full of peace, hope, and joy. Today is the best time to make the first step of moving on and moving forward. I would like to share with you one simple act that helped me cultivate self-compassion and forgiveness. Writing a forgiveness letter to yourself is a positive approach toward self-love that can lead each one of us to release unresolved anger that might have been weighing us down for years.

Dear me,

When God created you, you showed up along with my body. Since that time, you have never left me alone. You are fearfully and wonderfully made by God.

Perhaps I did not do a great job in protecting you. I confess that, many times, I was involved in crushing you. Maybe life was unfair, but I admit that I was not taking full ownership of you. I have not treated you with the love and respect you deserve. Your peace was not on top of my priorities. I cared deeply about everyone but you. I admit that I allowed you to suffer by letting people and circumstance control your peace. I am truly sorry. Would you please forgive me?

I am not proud of lots of things I did in the past. That is okay though. I did what I knew. Today I am a wiser person and know better. I promise to take better care of you. If I lose something I love or someone I deeply respect, I will not blame you and let you suffer. I will be grateful and patient. I will trust my God's wisdom and remind myself of His words: "... But perhaps you hate a thing and it is good for you; and perhaps you love a thing and it is bad for you. And Allah knows, while you know not" (Al-Baqarah 2:216).

I would like to thank you for being patient with me and never giving up on me. Thank you for understanding that I am just human and not perfect. I cannot promise you that I will not ever make mistakes. Nevertheless, I assure you that I will turn each mistake I made into a positive learning and growing experience.

Can I tell you something? You are such a lovely and beautiful soul, and I truly love you. You deserve peace, love, and affection. People often say to me that I am a kind person. From now on, I will let you touch my kindness before others. Your inner peace will be my priority. Even though I cannot see you with my naked eye, I would like to share with you the truth: I cannot live without you.

Lots of love,
Me

CHAPTER 9

The Power of Silence

The world is full of noise. Whether we are at home, work, school, or a shopping mall, there is always disruption. With the distraction of tech devices, emails, phone calls, and instant messages, our world is getting louder. We falsely think that in order to survive and prove that we are effective members in our society, we must belong to a busy and noisy environment. Unfortunately, for some of us, just being alone is not something ordinary or recommended, as it makes us feel nonfunctional or isolated. As a result of all these unnatural noises that have been created by humans, we end up feeling preoccupied, anxious, and irritable. We should take time to rest from these noises.

We are doing a great job managing our lives most of the time. We make time to go to work, spend time with family members, chat with friends, study, eat, sleep, exercise, play, and so on. Yet we often ignore the time to embrace silence. Without practicing the art of silence, we cannot succeed in this life. The time for silence must be added to our to-do list. Unfortunately, most of us engage in listening only to think of what we want to say when it is our turn to speak. Embracing silence while listening could be an opportunity to enhance our ability to stay focused. Listening effectively is also a great method that can provide to us new knowledge from the speakers. "… a time to keep silence, and a time to speak" (Ecclesiastes 3:7).

"Speech is silver, silence is golden" is a famous idiom that honors the value of silence. Communication with people can sometimes create some misunderstandings and conflicts that can cause us problems. In such cases, as believers, the best thing to do is to remain silent and trust that God is our Vindicator, as suggested by the following scriptures:

Indeed, Allah defends those who have believed ... (Al-Haj 22:38)

Those who guard their mouths, and their tongues keep themselves from calamity. (Proverbs 21:23)

The Lord will fight for you; you need only to be still. (Exodus 14:14)

Likewise, we sometimes face some people who insult or mistreat us, and we feel that we need to defend ourselves. For instance, when Mary gave birth to Jesus, God commanded her to remain silent in the face of anyone who would ask her concerning this matter. "So eat and drink and be contented. And if you see from among humanity anyone, say, 'Indeed, I have vowed to the Most Merciful abstention, so I will not speak today to [any] man'" (Maryam 19:26).

We human beings tend to over analyze the problems we face. We feed our problems by constantly talking about them with others, hoping they can provide solutions to our problems. However, there is a principle in life that goes, "What we focus on grows." Hence, the problem itself will grow instead of being solved. Instead of asking others what to do, we should practice being ourselves and listen to our inner voice, our intuition. We should allow our divine source, the Almighty God, to help us. Being silent in this case is an act of wisdom. "Even fools are thought wise if they keep silent, and discerning if they hold their tongues" (Proverbs 17:28).

In addition to the previously mentioned benefits, silence is a great treatment to boost our physical and mental well-being. By practicing silence, we can reduce our anxiety and stress levels, which in turn can reflect on our mood, immune system, and energy levels.

Silence is an art. Praying (or mediation) is one of the most effective ways to help us master this art. We must learn how to manage our busy schedule so we can spend some quality time alone with God, away from the distractions of this world. Why not make it a daily habit? In fact, praying alone in a quiet room will give us the opportunity to have a deeper understanding of God and strengthen our relationship with Him. In fact, it is only when the soul Is in harmony with its source that we can achieve the inner peace level and quiet our minds from the noise of the world.

Observing nature is another approach to mastering silence. Being surrounded by plants, trees, birds, and forest will teach us how to see the world from a different perspective. It is amazing how, from a tiny seed planted in soil, with the proper nutrition and environment, a tall tree that produces fruit grows. The process of growth here undergoes many transformations in which patience is required to move from one phase to another. From now on, whenever you see a tree, remember that one day that tree was a seed. This principle is also applicable to us. We are just like a seed. Tomorrow we could be like a tree if we were to quiet our minds, embrace patience, and apply the proper nutrition and environment. "That person is like a tree planted by streams of water, which its fruits in season and whose leaf does not wither whatever they do prospers" (Psalm 1:3). Water is another example from nature that can teach us how to be quiet, soft, gentle, and flexible. Have you ever seen the flow of water in a river? When you pass by a river or a stream, observe the behavior of water. You will find that water never resists any force or conflict. In fact, it always takes the easiest path. When water flows toward a large rock, it never tries to force the rock to move away. It flows gently and quietly around the rock and then continues its path. Being immersed in nature will definitely help us live in the present and enjoy the world away from the noise and chaos.

Embracing silence is a great method to boost our physical and mental health. Praying, meditation, and observing nature can have huge impacts on our relaxation and serenity state, which in turn can help us refocus on the straight path and the purpose of this life.

CHAPTER 10
Developing Mental Toughness

All of us face challenges and adversities at times. If we do not take the right action, it is easy for us to get overwhelmed. The scope of this chapter is the development of mental toughness that will help us cope and bounce back from setbacks. It is a calling to thrive rather than just survive.

Can you think of a successful person? Well, how do you describe a successful person? In your opinion, what are the key traits of successful people? Most of us think of the most successful person as the smartest or the most talented person around. While intelligence and talent are important predictors of success, there is one major trait a successful person must have to succeed. This trait is known as mental toughness or resilience.

Merriam-Webster defines "mental" as "related to the mind," and "toughness" as "strong or capable of enduring strain and hardship." Therefore, mental toughness is the ability to stay strong emotionally and intellectually under pressure without giving up. The good news here is that, whether you are successful or not, it is never too late to start investing in yourself to become mentally strong. If we are interested in being successful people, cultivating a mental toughness is a must.

To start investing in ourselves and refining our characters and skills, we must first acknowledge our strengths and weaknesses. In fact, none of us are born with mental skills, so there is no need to feel bad if we are not where we want to be. However, accepting that fact and doing nothing about it to improve ourselves is a big mistake many of us fall into. Therefore, to become mentality strong, having a high self-awareness about our own mental quality is the first step. Next, we have to decide to invest in ourselves. Then we should educate ourselves and take advantage of all the available opportunities to develop and improve ourselves.

So what actions should be taken to stay effective, focused, and determined under immense pressure? Building resilience requires us to have a higher self-awareness of our thought patterns and actions. We need to stay away from self-doubt and fear, and instead we should focus on creating a positive mindset by practicing gratitude, positive self-talk, and positive imagery. Positive thinking will increase our self-esteem and foster our resilience even in the most difficult times. Even when we make mistakes, instead of beating ourselves up, we should look at our shortcomings as learning experiences and opportunities to gain wisdom and perspective.

We all may have heard about Thomas Edison, the famous American inventor. We heard about his many unsuccessful trials while he was working on inventing the lightbulb. He tried a plethora of methods that led to failure. Instead of giving up, he decided to look at his fruitless experiments from a positive perspective: "I have not failed. I've just found 10,000 ways that won't work."

Michael Jordan is another example of a resilient person who shows how repeated failure can lead to success. He said, "I've missed more than 9,000 shots in my career. I've lost almost 300 games. Twenty-six times I've been trusted to take the game-winning shot and missed. I've failed over and over and over again in my life. And that is why I succeed."

These people are great examples of dedication and self-discipline. They teach each one of us to never give up, keep pushing, and try new approaches till we reach our goals. Indeed, there are many other examples of successful and resilient people who prove that failure is nothing but a stepping-stone to success. All these successful people share the same quality of resilience.

If we are interested in building resilience, we must step out from our comfort zone. Here is one example: Imagine you are a runner training for a race. If you are someone who always seeks comfort and waits for the ideal weather, time, place, and so forth, you will be missing out, and your performance may not improve. On the other hand, if you are interested in building mental toughness, you must step out of your comfort zone and experience running in adverse conditions.

… Indeed, Allah will not change the condition of a people until they change what is in themselves … (Ar-Ra'ad 13:11)

Do not conform to the pattern of this world but be transformed by the renewing of your mind … (Romans 12:2)

According to these verses, we are in charge of improving ourselves. God will not change our conditions until we take the first step to change our thought processes. Indeed, the process is difficult and challenging. Nevertheless, knowing that our God, the Creator of the universe, is the ultimate source of power, will inspire us to stay connected with Him and ask for His guidance. As believers, we should never give up, even if we do not see a way out. The true believers are the ones who always look at tough situations in an optimistic way. They see the hope and the opportunity for them to grow and develop character in the face of challenges. Hence, we should remain strong and courageous all the time, regardless of circumstances, as described in the following scriptures:

O you who have believed, persevere and endure and remain stationed and fear Allah that you may be successful (Al' Imran 3:200).

… And if there should come to you guidance from Me— then whoever follows My guidance will neither go astray [in the world] nor suffer [in the Hereafter]. (Taha 20:123)

Have I not commanded you? Be strong and courageous. Do not be afraid; do not be discouraged, for the Lord your God will be with you wherever you go. (Joshua 1:9)

So do not fear, for I am with you; do not be dismayed, for I am your God. I will strengthen you and help you; I will uphold you with my righteous right hand. (Isaiah 41:10)

> Not only so, but we also glory in our sufferings, because we
> know that suffering produces perseverance; perseverance,
> character; and character, hope. (Romans 5:3–4)

We all have dreams and goals. We all strive to be successful and productive. It is never too late to start investing in ourselves. It is possible for each one of us to refine our mental skills. Seeking God's help, guidance, and strength will indeed help us remain focused and determined in the face of difficulties.

CHAPTER 11

The Power of "I Do Not Know"

This chapters sheds light on the benefits of being an open-minded person by acknowledging what we do not know, which will make us eager to learn new things.

How many times have you heard the expression "I do not know"? If someone asks you a question and you do not know the answer, do you try to make up an answer? Do you have a hard time saying, "I do not know"? The answers to these questions may vary from one person to another depending on where a person is on his or her path of awareness. Almost all of us are somehow brainwashed to provide a quick and confident answer as if it is a sign of intelligence and productivity. In fact, there is power in saying, "I do not know." Acknowledging one's ignorance is an art that requires skills, such as honesty, self-confidence, and humility.

The term "ignorance" is defined as a lack of knowledge. Being ignorant about a particular topic is not a bad quality. Human beings, by nature, are not perfect, and we all are very limited in knowledge. If we knew everything, the word "learn" would not exist. Being aware of our ignorance is by itself a bliss to us. Knowing that we do not have enough information about a certain topic could present an opportunity to seek knowledge and gain more skills. On the other hand, if we are not aware of our ignorance, then we will be swimming in an ocean of illusion that can lead us to a disaster. For instance, most of us are aware of our bodies' needs, so we do our best to take a good care of our physical bodies by eating healthy food and exercising. However, many of us are ignorant about our spiritual needs. Hence, our souls suffer and never achieve inner peace, as we are not feeding our spirits with the proper nutrition. Only when we nourish our spirits can we experience bliss and inner peace.

Practicing intellectual humility helps us to always be in a state of integrity and open-mindedness. It is a state of understanding of our limited knowledge and the openness to new ideas. In fact, people who are intellectually humble are very confident and courageous, and they feel comfortable saying "I do not know" when necessary. They are also humbly aware about the fact that the more knowledge they receive, the more they realize how much they do not know. In contrast, arrogant people presume that they are correct all the time, are better than everyone else, and know more than others.

"Recite in the name of your Lord who created" (Al'Alaq 96:1). This is the first verse in the Holy Koran that encourages people to seek knowledge. This verse stresses the value of reading, studying, reflecting, and investigating. While God highly encourages His believers to seek knowledge, He discourages them from remaining in a state of ignorance. "… Say, 'Are those who know equal to those who do not know?' Only they will remember [who are] people of understanding" (Az-Zumar 39:9).

Seeking knowledge is indeed vital, and we must all look forward to it. Nevertheless, applying the knowledge we have into our lives is even more important. Again, by practicing intellectual humility, we will be able to use our knowledge and turn it into actions, which in turn can add meaning and perspective to our lives. In other words, we become wiser people. In fact, God gives wisdom to whom He wills, as the following scriptures illustrate:

> He gives wisdom to whom He wills, and whoever has been given wisdom has certainly been given much good. And none will remember except those of understanding. (Al-Baqarah 2:269)

> … He gives wisdom to the wise and knowledge to discerning. (Daniel 2:21)

> Having wisdom will help us remain in peace and pleasure at all times, even when we face challenges and trials in

our lives. It is truly a valuable gift from God. Therefore, we should constantly seek God's help and guidance to become wiser:

Call to me and I will answer you and tell you great and unsearchable things you do not know. (Jeremiah 33:3)

If any of you lacks wisdom, you should ask God, who gives generously to all without finding fault, and it will be given to you. (James 1:5)

Being aware of our ignorance will definitely be the driving force to seek more knowledge. Being intellectual and humble and seeking God's help and guidance will indeed help us become better people in all aspects of our lives. From now on, when you come across a question that you do not know the answer to, do not hesitate to say, "I do not know."

CHAPTER 12

Refuse to Have a Victim Mentality

This chapter focuses on the need to develop an awareness of our thoughts and attitudes that drive our moods and influence our behaviors. It urges us to take full responsibility for our actions.

Whether physically or emotionally, have you ever felt insulted, fooled, harmed, or attacked? Have you ever asked yourself, "Why me?" or "Why is the whole world is against me?" At some point in our lives, we all fall into the victim mentality and taste its negative impacts on our lives. While it is okay to acknowledge the suffering and the negative emotions that accompany such experiences for the sake of learning and growing, it is not okay, and it is not healthy to hang on to those feelings for long periods of time. Today we are going to choose to take great care of ourselves. We are going to say goodbye to the victim mentality and instead welcome the victor mentality into our lives.

Self-victimization is a choice we make every time we get attacked or treated unfairly by another person, culture, country, and the like. People with the victim mentality tend to constantly have negative self-talk and a lack of self-esteem. They feel powerless to change the situation, and they complain about the situation instead of trying to fix it, blame others, and never take full responsibility for their own actions. People with this victimized mindset always feel frustrated and angry, which in turn can negatively affect overall physical and mental health. Having a victim mentality is indeed an unpleasant experience that will impact not only us but also the people around us. Being aware about our destructive mindset and its negative impacts is the first step to be taken toward overcoming the victim mentality.

We have spent enough time complaining about our bad situations and blaming everyone, including ourselves, for the troubles we are facing. Is it not enough? Is it not time to move on and move forward? Is it not time to take care of ourselves? Is it not time to be set free from the victim mentality? Yes, it is the time!

- It is time to say no when we feel obligated to say yes or afraid of saying no.
- It is time to say no to anyone who is using us.
- It is time to say no to an unfair situation.
- It is time to say no to ourselves if we have been dwelling on the past.
- It is time to say no to ourselves if we have been blaming or criticizing others.
- It is time to say no to ourselves if we have been setting high expectations of ourselves based on the input of others.

No matter what may have caused us to obtain the victim mentality, it is time to take full responsibility to get out of it. Every one of us should have the mindset of "No one owes me anything."

To make this modification, we must forgive the people who harmed us, including ourselves. Although it is healthier to forget our past mistakes, it is important to remember the lessons learned so we do not repeat the same mistakes again. Being grateful for our past mistakes is a good approach to turn our failure times into learning opportunities, as it will allow us to grow and become wiser. Along with forgiveness and practicing gratitude, serving others is a great strategy to help us overcome this mindset. We all have talents we can share with others. It is a good feeling to know that each of us has the power to help someone.

The fastest path to eliminate our victim mentality is to turn to God with our suffering. When we keep the remembrance of God and allow Him to do work in our lives, He will help and guide us to set ourselves free from this toxic mindset. In fact, only God can turn our victim experience into a glorious experience. Knowing that we are not alone and believing that there is a purpose in our pain will indeed give us hope to get up on our feet.

> So do not weaken and do not grieve, and you will be superior if you are [true] believers. (Ali 'Imran 3:139)

> So do not fear, for I am with you; do not be dismayed, for I am your God. I will strengthen you and help you; I will uphold you with my righteous right hand. (Isaiah 41:10)

Let us take a moment to pause and reflect on these scriptures. How could it be possible for a true believer to have a victim mentality? If we are true believers, a destructive mindset cannot be part of our identities. During the unfair events, trials, and adversities, we all fall and struggle. But we should not give up, because we know that we are never alone. Being true believers means feeling the presence of God as a protector in every aspect in our lives. Being aware that God is our Vindicator and the only one who can pay us back for all the unfair things that happened to us will help us stand firm and trust His plan.

> And fear a Day when you will be returned to Allah. Then every soul will be compensated for what it earned, and they will not be treated unjustly. (Al-Baqarah 2:281)

> God will repay each person according to what they have done. (Romans 2:6)

Indeed, we all suffer in this life, and none of us are exempt from pain. However, being either a victim or a victor is a choice. It is up to each one of us to decide which path to take. You can stay where you are, complaining about the bad situation, blaming others, and playing the victim role. Or you can access your awareness and decide to take the right actions to free yourself to become a victor. Because it is always your choice, refuse to have a victim mentality!

CHAPTER 13

It Is Just a Habit

Having a higher self-awareness in identifying our habits is a blessing. This chapter offers an opportunity to improve the quality of our lives by replacing unhealthy habits with healthy habits.

Do you consider yourself an impulsive person? Are you aware of the way you speak? Do your words motivate or discourage others? At a certain point in our lives, we all follow the pattern of acting without thinking. For instance, many of us spend most of the day at our desks without thinking to take a small break. Whether it is positive or negative, it turns out that when we do one thing and repeat it often, it becomes a habit. While all of us have some good habits that we would like to possess, almost all of us have some bad habits that can have negative impacts on us and, in some cases, on others as well.

Changing our habits is not an easy task; it is a process that requires perseverance and patience. Therefore, we should never expect an overnight result. To see the desired results, we should always consider taking small and consistent steps. It is a safe process where we can see daily progress that motivates us to keep moving forward, one step at a time, without the fear or the worry of not completing our goals. On the other hand, if we do not take small steps, whenever we look at our goals, we will get overwhelmed and will eventually give up.

To replace an old habit, we should consider having a well-written plan—a solid plan that identifies each bad habit and addresses the following questions: Why it is a bad habit? How can I replace it with a better one? Along the process, what should I do if I feel overwhelmed and pressured to go back to the old habit? As an example, some of us have a bad habit of overeating junk food and drinking soda. In order to put an end to this habit, we must be conscious of the negative impacts of this habit on our overall health, such as having a high risk of obesity, depression, stress, type 2 diabetes, and so on. Then we should ask ourselves, "What causes us to overeat?" Next, it is important to visualize our future as if we have already succeeded in quitting that habit and become healthy and active people. Recall that to reach any goal, we must take baby steps and always start with one single step. In our case here, we probably can start by cutting the soda from our diet and drinking more water. Later, after two to three weeks, we can add another step, such as introducing more fruits and healthy snacks instead of junk food. To see a faster result, we should add some sort of exercise on a regular basis, such as walking, running, biking, etc. What also helps here is to find someone who shares a similar problem so we can motivate each other. Perhaps we can work out together and celebrate our victories together. It is important to mention here that the path to achieving any goal is not a straight line, and we should expect some setbacks and challenges. Therefore, if for any reason we screw up by missing a workout or eating unhealthy food, we should not panic. We should kindly forgive ourselves and attempt to regain access to the path.

Whatever the bad habit is, whether it is overeating unhealthy food, addiction to smartphones, smoking, or drinking, each one of us must be aware of it and take the proper actions to put an end to it. Nowadays there are plenty of available resources that teach us how to break an old habit. Also, we can get a great deal of motivation from others. There are numerous inspiring and supportive stories out there from people who have been through the same situation and succeeded in changing their bad habits.

Fasting is one of the potent spiritual methods that can help us break some of our bad habits. For instance, during the month of Ramadan, Muslims fast for thirty days from dawn to sunset. They refrain from eating any food, drinking any liquids, smoking, and engaging in any sexual activity. (There are some cases where people are excused from fasting, such as people who are ill, pregnant, breastfeeding, menstruating, or traveling, as well as young children and the elderly.). Similarly, in Christianity, there are several forms of fasting observed among many Christians, depending on the denomination they belong to. For instance, the Lenten fast is observed by the Roman Catholic Church and the Eastern Orthodox Church. The term "Lent" here refers to the period of forty days before Easter. During the Lenten fast, Christians abstain from consuming meat on Ash Wednesday and Good Friday, and they abstain from consuming meat on all Fridays during Lent. There are many other religions and belief systems that practice fasting in various ways as well. Fasting is an opportunity for us to detoxify our bodies and to cleanse our souls. Indeed, it is a powerful method to train ourselves to practice breaking certain habits.

Changing our old habits is a challenging process. However, by seeking God's help through prayer and patience, the path will become easier. "O you who have believed, seek help through patience and prayer. Indeed, Allah is with the patient" (Al-Baqarah 2:153). Whether consciously or unconsciously, at some point we all commit sins, such as negative assumptions or doubts about one another, spying on each other, gossiping, and saying bad things about others. If we do not take the suitable actions to stop them, these bad habits can have negative impacts on our physical and mental health. God already promised us that if we repent and seek His forgiveness for our sins, we will receive His forgiveness and His mercy.

> O you who have believed, avoid much [negative] assumption. Indeed, some assumption is sin. And do not spy or backbite each other. Would one of you like to eat the flesh of his brother when dead? You would detest it. And fear Allah; indeed, Allah is Accepting of repentance and Merciful. (Al-Hujurat 49:12)

> And when those come to you who believe in Our verses, say, "Peace be upon you. Your Lord has decreed upon Himself mercy: that any of you who does wrong out of ignorance and then repents after that and corrects himself—indeed, He is Forgiving and Merciful." (Al-An'am 6:54)

> Whoever conceals their sins does not prosper, but the one who confesses and renounces them finds mercy. (Proverbs 28:13)

Why not make a new daily habit of being grateful? Make your own gratitude journal; there is no need to share it with anyone. On a daily basis, spend ten to fifteen minutes thinking of three to five things you are grateful for. Then write your list down (or type it). Each one of us has unlimited gifts. "And if you should count the favors of Allah, you could not enumerate them. Indeed, Allah is Forgiving and Merciful" (An-Nahl 16:18). Can we start looking at the people in our lives as gifts—people like parents, kids, spouses, siblings, and friends? What about our jobs, health, cars, and phones? Let us pause here for a moment and just ponder our own organs and systems in our bodies. Have we ever thought to thank God for gifting us the bones and the joints that allow us to move and stand? Can we stop taking things for granted?

- If you have a house, whenever you enter your house, say, "Thank God," because there are many homeless people around the world who cannot afford to pay for rent.
- If you are feeling healthy and able to walk, say, "Thank God," because there are many sick people who cannot even move.
- If you can see and enjoy the beauty of nature and listen to the birds, say, "Thank God," because there are many people cannot hear or see anything.
- If you are facing challenges and struggles today, say, "Thank God," because God is training you to build resilience and character.

Thanking God all the time is a positive habit. By embracing gratitude daily, we can shift our attention to being consistently focused on the positive emotions. This is a method that has a huge impact on our overall health and happiness as well.

Improving our habits is the best investment we can ever make in our lives. Yes, it is a challenging process and requires lots of conscious work from our end. But it is possible, and we can all do it. Always remember that it is never too late to start developing new habits and getting rid of some old ones. Why not be one of the people who are going to decide to take some action today and start investing in themselves? Always remember that it is just a habit and it does not define you!

CHAPTER 14

Humility

This chapter sheds light on the power of humility. Before introducing the term "humility," I would like to open this chapter by asking the following questions: Do you really care about others as you care about yourself? How do you react when someone criticizes you? Do you always see yourself as a strong and capable person? Nobody likes arrogant people. Guess what? We do not view ourselves as arrogant, but at some point in our lives, our behaviors and actions show arrogant tendencies. There is bad and good news here. The bad news is that sometimes our behaviors and actions can have negative impacts on others, and we are not aware of that. The good news is that we can train ourselves to be humble by constantly watching our behaviors and actions. Really, it is all about mindfulness.

Merriam-Webster defines "humility" as "freedom from pride or arrogance." To be a humble person is to be an authentic human being who treats everyone with respect, lives in harmony with everyone, and believes that we all are equal regardless of our status or background. To be a humble person is to be a peacemaker on this planet.

> And the servants of the Most Merciful are those who walk upon the earth easily, and when the ignorant address them [harshly], they say [words of] peace. (Al-Furqan 25:63)

> Live in harmony with one another. Do not be proud but be willing to associate with people of low position. Do not be conceited. (Romans 12:16)

Let us think about the most influential people in history. There is no need to mention any names here, because each one of us already has a list of names. All of us agree that all the greatest people are the most humble ones. They are the people who work hard without waiting for approval or compliments from others—not because they think so highly about themselves, but because they focus on serving others and not on their egos. They simply remove their self-concerns from the equation.

When someone dies, it is very common for Muslims to recite this verse: "… Indeed, we belong to Allah, and indeed to Him we will return" (Al-Baqarah 2:156). In fact, this verse should be recited oftentimes. We should always remind ourselves that everything we have is a gift from God. Being a humble servant means being grateful to Almighty God all the time. Even when we give in charity, we should be grateful to God, who prepared the opportunity for us to do something good. By praying, seeking God's face, and turning away from our wicked ways, we will be able to receive His grace and forgiveness, and He will answer our prayers:

> Indeed, they who have believed and done righteous deeds and humbled themselves to their Lord—those are the companions of Paradise; they will abide eternally therein. (Hud 11:23)

> Certainly will the believers have succeeded: They who are during their prayer humbly submissive. (Al-Mu'minun 23:1–2)

> … God opposes the proud but shows favor to the humble. (James 4:6)

> If my people, who are called by my name, will humble themselves and pray and seek my face, and turn from their wicked ways; then will I hear from heaven, and I will forgive their sin, and will heal their land. (2 Chronicles 7:14)

To be humble to God is to put yourself at the lowest position before God. For instance, during prayers, Muslims prostrate themselves on the ground. It is not only a physical act; it is a spiritual act as well. Physically, they touch their foreheads to the ground. Spiritually, they connect their hearts to the Creator of the entire universe. It is an act that acknowledges humility before the Almighty. It is a position where someone can tell God all his or her needs and desires. It is a position where someone is at the closest position to God. "... But prostrate and draw near [to Allah]" (Al-Alaq 96:19). In addition to the spiritual benefits, prostration can boost alpha brain waves, which in turn can increase relaxation and reduce tension. What a great free-of-cost medication!

To show unworthiness and humility to God, there is no position better than to put our foreheads down to the ground before God. The following scriptures illustrate how the prophets fell on their faces to show humility to God:

> Those were the ones upon whom Allah bestowed favor from among the prophets of the descendants of Adam and of those We carried [in the ship] with Noah, and of the descendants of Abraham and Israel [i.e., Jacob], and of those whom We guided and chose. When the verses of the Most Merciful were recited to them, they fell in prostration and weeping. (Maryam 19:58)

> Going a little farther, he fell with his face to the ground and prayed, 'My Father, if it is possible, may this cup be taken from me. Yet not as I will, but as you will. (Matthew 26:39)

> Moses bowed to the ground at once and worshiped. (Exodus 34:8)

> Abram fell facedown, and God said to him, "As for me, this is my covenant with you: You will be the father of many nations." (Genesis 17:3–4)

> ... Then Joshua fell facedown to the ground in reverence ... (Joshua 5:14)

How could I end this chapter without mentioning parents? Our parents are the only people on this planet who love us unconditionally. They are the only people who really want the best for us. Our parents are the people who deserve our love, respect, and mercy. The following scriptures emphasize the importance of honoring our parents:

> And your Lord has decreed that you worship not except Him, and to parents, good treatment. Whether one or both of them reach old age [while] with you, say not to them [so much as], "uff," and do not repel them but speak to them a noble word—And lower to them the wing of humility out of mercy and say, "My Lord, have mercy upon them as they brought me up [when I was] small." (Al-Isra 17:23–24)

> Honor your father and your mother, as the Lord your God commanded you ... (Deuteronomy 5:16)

Being a humble person means being a person who believes that he or she is not better than others and that we all need to help each other. Being humble means acknowledging our weaknesses and unworthiness to God and asking Him for His help and mercy. Today let us be honest with ourselves, let us watch our behaviors and actions, and let each one of us ask the following question: "Am I truly a humble person?"

CHAPTER 15

Choose to Be Positive

There is incredible power in our words and thoughts. When we repeat them, they will sink into our subconscious mind, and eventually they will influence our behaviors and actions. This chapter urges us to be mindful of our words and actions, which can shape our lives.

Have you ever seen a child throwing a stone in the water? As soon as the stone hits the surface, a ripple effect takes place. It is interesting how a small ring of water around the stone can create larger circular rings that travel outward. In fact, the principle of the ripple effect can also be applied to our actions and reactions. Every tiny action or reaction, whether it is positive or negative, is going to impact us and others. Hence, it is our responsibility to control our own actions and reactions.

A good and positive word has a solid foundation and has the power to inspire us and uplift our moods. On the other hand, a negative word has no foundation, and it has the power to harm us and destroy our souls. We must be mindful of how we select our words. In fact, by selecting the right words, with a sincere heart and good intention, we have the power to heal a broken heart. The following scriptures highlight the influence of our words on ourselves and others:

> Have you not considered how Allah presents an example, a good word like a good tree, whose root is firmly fixed and its branches [high] in the sky? It produces its fruit all the time, by permission of its Lord. And Allah presents examples for the people that perhaps they will be

reminded. And the example of a bad word is like a bad tree, uprooted from the surface of the earth, not having any stability. (Ibrahim 14:24–26)

Kind speech and forgiveness are better than charity followed by injury … (Al-Baqarah 2:263)

The soothing tongue is a tree of life, but a perverse tongue crushes the spirit. (Proverbs 15:4)

Gracious words are a honeycomb, sweet to the soul and healing to the bones. (Proverbs 16:24)

Almost all of us have lost something we desire at some point in our lives. During such a time, we experienced the feeling of devastation. For instance, if we get laid off from work, most of us tend to think and feel negatively. However, after finding a new job, we realize that being laid off was the best thing that could have happened to us, as it allowed us to move forward and get a better job. While facing a challenging situation, it is very important to practice being an open-minded person. Being aware of the pattern of our self-talk is very important. While negative thoughts can negatively affect our mental and physical health, practicing self-compassion is the right approach in this tough situation. We should gently and kindly speak to ourselves as if we are speaking to our best friends. For instance, let us examine the case of being laid off from a job. Following are some examples of how we could switch our self-talk from negative to positive in such a scenario:

Negative Self-Talk Examples

- I feel like a failure, and no one will ever hire me.
- There is no way it will ever work out for me.
- I am not smart and dedicated enough to achieve my goals.
- With my luck, I will never get a job.
- I do not have enough skills and experience.
- I have no more purpose in my life.

Positive Self-Talk Examples

- Although I do not know why I got laid off, I am positive that this will be an opportunity to get my dream job.
- Yes, I lost my job, but I definitely gained new skills and experience that will lead me to get a better job.
- Today I am facing difficult challenges, but I trust God's plan.
- Everything happened for a reason, and it is all good.
- I will do what I can, and God will do what I cannot.
- When I find a job, I will go to someone who has been laid off, and I will tell that person, "You will get through this. I have been there, and with the help of God, I made it."

Because of our lack of knowledge and wisdom, we sometimes like things that are bad for us and hate things that are good for us. On the other hand, God is perfect in His knowledge and wisdom, and He sometimes allows things to happen to us because it is good for us, as they will shape us and make us stronger. So when we lose something, we must remind ourselves that everything will work out for our good. That is exactly what the divine Creator clarifies in His words:

> ... But perhaps you hate a thing and it is good for you; and perhaps you love a thing and it is bad for you. And Allah Knows, while you know not. (Al-Baqarah 2:216)

> And we know that in all things God works for the good of those who love him, who have been called according to his purpose. (Romans 8:28)

As believers, when things seem to be out of control, we should not panic. In fact, when we rely only on God and not on our abilities or the people we know, God promises to make a way out for us, even if there seems to be no way. He will also provide for us all our needs in ways we will not expect.

> ... And whoever fears Allah—He will make for him a way out—And He will provide for him from where he does

not expect. And whoever relies upon Allah—then He is sufficient for him. Indeed, Allah will accomplish His purpose. Allah has already set for everything a [decreed] extent. (At-Talaq 65:2–3)

... I am making a way in the wilderness and streams in the wasteland. (Isaiah 43:19)

Practicing gratitude is one of the most powerful ways that enable us to see the world from a positive perspective. If we want more things to show up in our lives, we must be thankful for all we already have. This is a prescription given by our God to each one of us. "... If you are grateful, I will surely increase you [in favor] ..." (Ibrahim 14:7). Gratitude is a free-of-cost medicine that is highly recommended for our overall physical and mental health. It has been shown that gratitude helps lower levels of cortisol, the primary stress hormone in our bodies. Generally speaking, people with positive attitudes are happier and have healthier relationships with others. Compared to others, positive people have higher confidence, stronger immune systems, lower blood pressure, less risk of heart disease, less stress, less anxiety, and so on.

To see the positive change in the universe, the principle of the ripple effect of our words and actions must be applied. Never underestimate any word or any small action. You never know; one simple act of kindness from your sincere heart might make a huge difference in the lives of others, even if you do not see it. It is your choice to decide what you want to send to the universe. Why not be the person who spreads the positive vibes to others? Why not be the person who decides to let someone smile today? It is your choice. Make sure to choose to be positive!

CHAPTER 16

The Joy of Giving

Since we were kids, we have been experiencing the joy of receiving gifts on various occasions, such as birthdays, graduations, holidays, and weddings. What makes it a good feeling is the idea that the giver is thinking of us. Before opening a gift, we tend to put beautiful smiles on our faces to show our gratitude to the giver. The older we get, the more we realize how important it is to appreciate the gifts and the givers. Receiving a gift will indeed brighten our day and bring us joy. However, the act of giving makes us much happier than the act of receiving. When we give from a sincere heart with the intention of making a difference in another person's life without expecting anything in return, we are truly adding meaning, fulfillment, and joy to our lives. Mother Teresa once stated, "It's not how much we give but how much love we put into giving." Indeed, giving is an act of love and compassion. "[Saying], 'We feed you only for the countenance of Allah. We wish not from you reward or gratitude'" (Al-Insan 76:9).

The concept of charity is universal. Whether it is obligatory charity from God or volunteer charity, charitable acts of giving are very beneficial to us, as the following scriptures illustrate:

> The example of those who spend their wealth in the way of Allah is like a seed [of grain] which grows seven spikes; in each spike is a hundred grains. And Allah multiplies [His reward] for whom He wills. And Allah is all-Encompassing and knowing. (Al-Baqarah 2:261)

> Those who spend their wealth [in Allah's way'] by night and by day, secretly and publicly—they will have their reward with the Lord. And no fear will there be concerning them, nor will they grieve. (Al-Baqarah 2:274)

> A generous person will prosper; whoever refreshes others will be refreshed. (Proverbs 11:25)

> And if anyone gives even a cup of cold water to one of these little ones who is my disciple, truly I tell you, that person will certainly not lose their reward. (Matthew 10:42)

By giving charitably, we are not only helping others, but we are also helping ourselves by earning God's reward. Whatever we spend in charity will never be lost. It will be replaced and multiplied by the Almighty. As a reward of this act, the believer will always embrace the joy away from fear and grief. By giving charitably, we can have a great and safe investment for eternity.

When we think about the word "give," the first thing that often comes to our minds is the word "money." Although it is very important to give money to help people in need, organizations, and religious institutions, not everyone has enough money to spare. There are many ways to practice the art of giving. "Each of you should use whatever gift you have received to serve others, as faithful stewards of God's grace in its various forms" (1 Peter 4:10). For instance, our time is one of the most precious gifts. Maybe you are a good listener and you can offer a listening ear to someone in need. Sometimes just being with someone who needs support is highly rewarding. Perhaps you can take few hours from your busy schedule to volunteer with a charitable organization. Knowledge and skills can also be some of the greatest gifts someone can share with others. Some of us do not have enough time to teach or volunteer for hours, but why not share a short story from your own life experiences?

Maybe you went through painful experiences that have taught you a great deal. Today you consider yourself a wise person, and you would like to make a difference in someone else's life. Why not start writing your own book to share your wisdom with others for the sake of helping and inspiring others?

Besides all these gifts that can be shared with others, there is an incredible free-of-cost gift that is available to everyone and can be used anytime and anywhere. A smile is a simple act we can offer to the world and to ourselves. It can brighten not only our souls but also the souls of others. By smiling we can create a positive environment that can lift the spirits and moods of those around us. By keeping smiles on our faces, we inspire others to smile as well.

It is very important to mention here that every tiny action we take will create a ripple effect. There is a powerful scripture in the Holy Koran that highlights the power of a tiny action: "So whoever does an atom's weight of good will see it—And whoever does an atom's weight of evil will see it" (Az-Zalzalah 99:7–8). From now on, every time we intend to take one simple action or say one word, let us ask ourselves, "Do I really have to say this word? Is this word (or action) going to hurt someone's feeling? Is it going to put a smile on someone's face?" Do whatever you want; it is your choice. But make sure to pick a good attitude.

Because we all are connected, let us choose to practice giving for the sake of spreading love and kindness to the world, and it will come back to us. It is a promise! We all have gifts and talents that we can share with others. Let us all practice the art of giving and enjoy its blessing and joy with everyone.

CHAPTER 17

Moderation in Everything

Water is life! Every living thing is made of water. "Have those who disbelieved not considered that the heavens and the earth were a joined entity, and then We separated them and made from water every living thing? ..." (Al-Anbiya 21:30). Without water, no human being, animal, or plant can survive. Hence, drinking an adequate amount of water is very important and essential to our health. However, drinking too much water can be dangerous. Overhydration can lead to water intoxication, which is characterized by a low sodium level in the blood. Moderation in diet and nutrition is the best approach for us to stay healthy.

> ... Eat and drink, but be not excessive. Indeed, He likes not those who commit excess. (Al-A'raf 7:31)

> If you find honey, eat just enough—too much of it, and you will vomit. (Proverbs 25:16)

Too much water is also bad for most trees and plants. If the soil of a plant is constantly wet, there will be not enough air in the soil, and the plant cannot take in oxygen. So a plant needs just enough water to stay healthy. Similarly, moderation in all aspects of life leads to a healthy and fulfilling existence.

"There is a time for everything, and a season for every activity under the heavens" (Ecclesiastes 3:1). Because there is a time for everything, we need to create balance between personal and professional life. We should always remind ourselves that we do not live to work, but we work to live.

Let us be mindful of how we are living. We should consider moderation in our daily activities, such as working, parenting, meditating, and so on. It is important to mention here that being a believer does not mean withdrawing from this worldly life and just focusing on praying and the hereafter. In fact, we should live and enjoy this earthly life and use it so we can have a good life here *and* in the hereafter. Let us consider the following scripture, which encourages people to balance between the world and the hereafter. "But seek, through that which Allah has given you, the home of the Hereafter; and [yet], do not forget your share of the world ..." (Al-Qasas 28:77).

Moderation in spending is a good example of this point. Being generous in spending money on ourselves, families, and relatives is a good quality someone can choose to have. Similarly, saving money is a good way to protect our future. Yet moderation is the key to keep us safe. Even when we intend to give charitably, moderation should be considered. Certainly, God wants us to help others and perform acts of kindness, such as giving charitably and doing righteous deeds. However, God also wants us to consider moderation because we should not harm ourselves and our dependents in the process:

> And [they are] those who, when they spend, do so not excessively or sparingly but are ever, between that, [justly] moderate. (Al-Furqan 25:67)

> A good person leaves an inheritance for their children's children ... (Proverbs 13:22)

We all have relationships with others, such as close friends and family members. Having balance in our relationships will make them healthy and keep us safe. In other words, we must learn how to love in moderation. Loving someone to an extreme or being attached to someone could be very dangerous to our health and well-being. If we love someone to the extreme, the moment we lose that person, we will feel that we lost the sense of our identity and security, and we will become emotionally depressed. Therefore, considering balance in our emotions is the best approach to keep our relationships healthy. Likewise, we should not hate anyone, even if we consider them an enemy. Maybe the person you are having a problem with today will be your beloved one in future. "Perhaps Allah will put, between you and those to whom you have been enemies among them, affection …" (Al-Mumtahanah 60:7).

The only relationship that does not require restraint is the relationship with the Almighty God. This is the only relationship that will never break our hearts. God is not like humans. He never ignores us or lets us down. He is the only one who can mend our broken hearts. If our intentions are pure, then our pain, our grief, and even our tears become means to earning blessings from our Lord. Even when we make mistakes and repent to Him, His door is always open, welcoming us and never rejecting us. He is God, the most merciful and the most loving!

> And ask forgiveness of your Lord and then repent to Him. Indeed, my Lord is Merciful and Affectionate. (Hud 11:90).

> Who is a God like you, who pardons sin and forgives the transgression of the remnant of his inheritance? You do not stay angry forever but delight to show mercy. You will again have compassion on us; you will tread our sins underfoot and hurl all our iniquities into the depths of the sea. (Micah 7:18–19)

Really, with God, we do not have to be concerned about moderation. The more we put our love into God, the more we will feel His love and security. The more we remember God, the more we will feel peace and joy. The more we talk to Him, the more we will feel His presence. The more we admit our weaknesses and embrace humility to Him, the more we will experience His power and strength in our lives. "… Love the Lord your God with all your heart and with all your soul and with all your strength and with all your mind …" (Luke 10:27).

Being a moderate and balanced person is not an easy task, and we cannot expect an overnight change. It is a process that requires lots of conscious effort and patience, as it forces us to continually observe our activities and behaviors. Here is the good news: when we invite balance into our lives, peace will be our reward. You can choose to be the best person with the best character traits, but never forget to be moderate in everything. Nevertheless, the only relationship in which you do not need to worry about moderation is your relationship with the Almighty God.

CHAPTER 18

There Is a Time for Everything

> There is a time for everything, and a season
> for every activity under the heavens,
> a time to be born and a time to die,
> a time to plant and a time to uproot,
> a time to kill and a time to heal,
> a time to tear down and a time to build,
> a time to weep and a time to laugh,
> a time to mourn and a time to dance,
> a time to scatter stones and a time to gather them,
> a time to embrace and a time to refrain from embracing,
> a time to search and a time to give up,
> a time to keep and a time to throw away,
> a time to tear and a time to mend,
> a time to be silent and a time to speak,
> a time to love and a time to hate,
> a time for war and a time for peace.
> —Ecclesiastes 3:1–8

There is a time for everything! What a powerful message from God for each one of us! Pondering on the above scripture will calm us and fill our hearts with peace and hope. These words inform us that nothing will last forever and everything is temporary. If we are crying and feeling sad today, it will not last forever. Tomorrow is coming, and we will smile again. Why? Because there is a time for everything.

We all have responsibilities toward our work, families, relatives, friends, communities, and so on. But sometimes we forget that there is a time for everything. We ignore the fact that we are in control of managing our daily tasks and activities, and we end up frustrated and exhausted. Because there is a time for everything, we must make time to take care of ourselves. If you do not love yourself and take care of your health and well-being, what makes you think that someone else will? Make sure to schedule time to invest in yourself. For instance, you can go for a walk or a run, read a book, take a nap, or just simply practice silence or meditation. Even during your lunchtime at work, try to not check your email, and tell yourself, "This is a time to eat my lunch."

Because there is a time for everything, there is a time to be tested. While we all enjoy the positive times when things go our way, no one enjoys the pain that is associated with the challenges and difficulties that we face in our lives when we are being tested.

> And We will surely test you with something of fear and hunger and a loss of wealth and lives and fruits ... (Al-Baqarah 2:155)

> See, I have refined you, though not as silver; I have tested you in the furnace of affliction. For my own sake, for my own sake, I do this ... (Isaiah 48:10–11)

Instead of complaining about the pain, we should accept the pain as part of the test and remind ourselves that it is only temporary. Plus we should always remember that there is a purpose for our pain. It is intended to bring us closer to God, purify our faith, wash away our sins, and make us stronger.

How can we seek help amid hardships? Through patience and prayer, we can overcome difficulties. This is powerful advice from God during the difficult seasons. "O you who have believed, seek help through patience and prayer. Indeed, Allah is with the patient" (Al-Baqarah 2:153). Because there is a time for everything, embracing patience is one of the most effective ways to accomplish any goal. For instance, when a woman goes through the stages of pregnancy, it is well known that she experiences pain, aches, depression, sadness, and hormonal changes. Imagine a pregnant woman who refuses to go through all these stages to avoid all kinds of pain associated with the process. If she decides to deliver her baby before the due date, the baby will not be healthy and might have a plethora of health complications. Therefore, to get the best outcome in anything we do, we have to be patient. The following verses highlight the importance of patience while we are in the process of achieving our goals:

> O you who have believed, persevere and endure and remain stationed and fear Allah that you may be successful. (Al'Imran 3:200)

> … So be patient; indeed, the [best] outcome is for the righteous. (Hud 11:49)

> The end of a matter is better than its beginning, and patience is better than pride. (Ecclesiastes 7:8)

> You too, be patient and stand firm, because the Lord's coming is near. (James 5:8)

Because there is a time for everything, we should always expect new beginnings in our lives. Unfortunately, many of us waste our time and energy on things and people we lost in the past, and we end up missing the present moments that could bring us many new opportunities. Maybe, for some reason, your friendship with a close friend ends, or maybe the person you love deeply disappears out of the blue. Maybe you are in a job you do not like and it is a time to consider a career change. Always remember that everything is temporary. Nevertheless, we should always expect new beginnings in this life. Perchance you are single and you are interested in getting married and having your own family. Maybe you are in the process of starting a new business or moving to a new house. Can we start allowing new beginnings to show up in our lives? That is exactly what Mother Nature is constantly teaching us:

- There is a time for the sun to rise and a time for the sun to set.
- There is a time for the flowers to blossom and a time for them to die.
- There is a time for a tree to be full of beautiful, new, and green leaves, and there is a time for the leaves to change their color and fall to the ground.
- There is a time to plant a fruit tree, a time to eat its fruit, and a time for the tree to die.
- There is a time to have a sunny and bright day and a time for a thunderstorm to take place.

Whatever you are facing today, always remember that nothing will last forever and everything is temporary. If things are going the way you like, that is awesome! Make sure to enjoy the good time with your loved ones. If you are experiencing anguish, remember that there is a purpose behind your sorrow. It is only temporary, and you will come out stronger and wiser. To achieve your goals and to remain calm along the road, never forget to seek help through prayer and patience. And never forget that there is a time for everything!

PART III

We All Are Spiritually Connected

The last part of this book emphasizes the importance of human connection. By controlling our thoughts and actions, we can choose to influence everyone around us. This part urges you to practice being an authentic human being that sees himself or herself in everyone he or she encounters. While reading this part, allow yourself to reflect on each chapter. Visualize yourself as the one who is uplifting others and extending love and compassion to you and all around you.

CHAPTER 19

Everything Is Connected

All matter was a single point with infinite density and intense heat until a massive explosion took place and gave birth to the universe. This event, the big bang, occurred about fourteen billion years ago. At that time, space expanded very quickly, and the energy of the big bang was evenly spread out through space, causing the universe to cool. Things such as the formation of atoms, stars, galaxies, planets, and human beings began to occur. Now, let us ask ourselves a few questions. For each question, please take a moment to pause and reflect. Can you imagine how life would be on Earth if the sun had not been created? Can you imagine a life with no water or oxygen? Absolutely, there is no life without the presence of our main needs. Now let us imagine that nothing is missing in the universe; however, you are the only human on this planet. Can you imagine what your life looks like? Everything in this universe, whether we see it or not, represents a fragment of the universe, and it was created by God for a specific purpose. As humans, we all are equally created by the Almighty God to be together and share our mercy and compassion with one another. We all walk on the same earth, breath the same air, and drink the same water. Indeed, we all are connected!

Now, let us have a look at the human body. There are eleven organ systems in the human body. Each body system has a specific function that keeps us healthy. To maintain equilibrium, our body systems must communicate and work together. For instance, to maintain a stable internal temperature, the cardiovascular, integumentary, respiratory, and muscular systems must work together. It is incredible how all our cells, vessels, and organs work together to keep us alive and healthy. If your heart stops pumping blood, do you think the other organs in your body can ignore that problem and keep you functioning? Everything in our bodies is connected. This is also true for our spirits; as soon as we get disconnected from our source, the spirit will become crushed, and we will feel distracted and frustrated. "And whoever turns away from My remembrance—indeed, he will have a depressed life …" (Taha 20:124).

Spending time in natural environments will indeed strengthen our connection with nature, which in turn can bring peace and healing into our lives. To enhance your connection with nature, it is recommended that you go for a nature walk and observe what is happening around you. Look at the trees and observe the design and the color of the leaves. Look at the beautiful flowers and their colors. Feel the fresh air and the sunshine. Listen to the sound of birds chirping and water running if possible. For every step you take, feel the ground. Notice the connection with the earth and feel its solidity. Exposure to nature will have positive effects on our emotional, mental, and physical well-being. Just being in nature will help us improve focus, live in the present moment, stimulate positive creativity, and appreciate the life that has been gifted to us. The next time you feel lonely or stressed, just go for a walk along a pretty nature trail near you and appreciate your surroundings. While walking and reflecting, do not forget to honor God, as everything has been exalting God, even if you do not understand their ways of exalting.

> The seven heavens and the earth and whatever is in them exalt Him. And there is not a thing except that it exalts [Allah] by His praise, but you do not understand their [way of] exalting. Indeed, He is ever Forbearing and Forgiving. (Al-Isra 17:44)

> But ask the animals, and they will teach you, or the birds in the sky, and they will tell you; or speak to the earth, and it will teach you, or let the fish in the sea inform you. Which of all these does not know that the hand of the Lord has done this? In his hand is the life of every creature and the breath of all mankind. (Job 12:7–10)

The quality of humans' relationships with each other will definitely have impacts on our overall mental health. For instance, imagine yourself holding a burning candle in a dark room. The flame of your candle lights that room. Now imagine there are more people with you in that same dark room, and each one of you is holding one candle. If all of the people help each other light all the candles, the light in the room will increase rapidly. That is exactly what will happen when we all treat each other as one family whose members show nothing but mercy and compassion for one another. We will create a healthy and peaceful environment that can continuously radiate tranquility where people live together in unity and harmony, away from hate, anger, and envy. That is truly how God wants us to live in this life:

> The believers are nothing but brothers, so make settlement between your brothers ... O mankind, indeed We have created you from male and female and made you peoples and tribes that you may know one another ... (Al-Hujurat 49:10, 13)

> How good and pleasant it is when God's people live together in unity! (Psalm 133:1)

> ... "Love your neighbor as yourself." There is none other commandment greater than these. (Mark 12:31)

We may come from different backgrounds and countries, follow different religions, and speak different languages. Nevertheless, we all are spiritual beings and want to be appreciated and treated with kindness. Can we stop judging others? Is it not time to practice humanity? Is it not time to acknowledge that everything is connected?

CHAPTER 20

Kindness: Our Golden Rule

...Do not worship except Allah; and to parents do good
and to relatives, orphans, and the needy. And speak to
people good [words] and establish prayer ...
—Al-Baqarah 2:83

Finally, all of you, be like-minded, be sympathetic, love
one another, be compassionate and humble.
—1 Peter 3:8

Would you please pause for a moment and read the above scriptures one more time? Is it not astonishing that our religions teach us to embrace kindness and respect toward others regardless of their education, money, or status? Yet we still perform acts of unkindness toward each other, even at the community level. Do we truly think that we are righteous believers? If we are believers, we should be kind and respectful to each other. Whether you are a Muslim, Christian, or someone who does not identify with any religion, we are all human beings. We all want to be treated with respect, compassion, and love.

Have you ever heard about the Golden Rule? It is a universal moral principle that is applicable to all mankind. It urges people to treat others the way they themselves would like to be treated. We all are equal in God's eyes. The most honored among us is the one who is most righteous. We all have our own version of the Golden Rule. Below are some examples of this universal rule from the religious scriptures of the world:

- Islam:

    O mankind, indeed We have created you from male and female and made you peoples and tribes that you may know one another. Indeed, the most noble of you in the sight of Allah is the most righteous of you. Indeed, Allah is Knowing and Acquainted. (Al-Hujurat 49:13)

    Worship Allah and associate nothing with Him, and to parents do good, and to relatives, orphans, the needy, the near neighbor, the neighbor farther away, the companion at your side, the traveler, and those whom your right hands possess. Indeed, Allah does not like those who are self-deluding and boastful. (Al-Nisa 4:36).

- Christianity:

    So in everything, do to others what you would have them to do to you, for this sums up the Law and the Prophets. (Matthew 7:12)

- Judaism:

    What is hateful to you, do not do to your neighbor. This is the whole Torah; all the rest is commentary. Go and learn it. (Talmud, Shabbath 31a)

- Buddhism:

    Treat not others in ways that you yourself would find hurtful. (Udana-Varga 5.18)

- Hindiusm:

    This is the sum of duty: do not do to others what would cause pain if done to you. (Mahabharata 5:151)

- Jainism:

One should treat all creatures in the world as one would like to be treated. (Mahavira Sutrakritanga 1.11.33)

We all are equals, and we should treat others the way we would like to be treated. Whether you are talking with a CEO or a janitor, there is no difference. Both are human beings and deserve to be treated with respect and dignity. Albert Einstein has a beautiful quote that delivers a similar message: "I speak to everyone in the same way, whether he is the garbage man or the president of the university."

Because there is power in small steps, let us decide today to take small steps to change the world through small acts of kindness. For instance, let us smile at people we meet, even if they are strangers. Maybe your smile is going to brighten someone's day. Let us make it a habit. Smiling at others will not only make us feel better but will enhance our relationships with others. Practicing gratitude is another act of kindness. Let us be grateful to someone who is simply holding the door open for us. Let us practice saying "Thank you" to a janitor, whose main job is to provide a cleaner environment to others. Although saying "Thank you" seems to be a very simple act, we often forget to thank the people who are constantly helping us in our lives.

If we purify our intentions and decide to be kind toward others, we can embrace kindness at anytime and anywhere. Because each action has its ripple effect, whatever we are going to offer to others today, they may offer it to someone else later. It is important to mention here that when we intend to do any action, we should not expect anything in return. Otherwise, we might get discouraged and frustrated by others. Hence, let us just do good for the sake of spreading kindness in our world without dependence on others reciprocating our good deeds. Embracing kindness is a way to obtain the ultimate reward from God:

... And do good; indeed, Allah loves the doers of good. (Al-Baqarah 2:195)

But love your enemies, do good to them, and lend to them without expecting to get anything back. Then your reward will be great ... (Luke 6:35)

While practicing kindness can reinforce our social connections, kindness can also boost our moods and overall well-being. Have you ever asked yourself why you feel good when you do something good? It is proven that when we practice kindness, our brains reward us by releasing several chemicals, such as oxytocin, serotonin, dopamine, and endorphins. These chemicals give us feelings of satisfaction and joy. For instance, oxytocin helps us in forming social bonds and trusting others, serotonin regulates our mood, dopamine is associated with happiness, and endorphins are natural painkillers. In addition to these benefits, performing acts of kindness can reduce levels of cortisol, the stress hormone, thereby lowering anxiety. It is incredible how a simple act of kindness can be a free-of-cost treatment for our pain, depression, and anxiety.

What a great idea it is to wake up each morning asking God to use each one of us as an instrument of peace and love to others. Today, decide to set a positive intention to help someone in need. Remember, we all have gifts and talents to share. Let us help each other and pray for each other. Because we are all connected, let us bloom where we are planted by spreading kindness to others.

CHAPTER 21

Praying for Peace and Love

N owadays, the entire world is facing health crises, including the COVID-19 pandemic, which has affected every single human on our planet; wars; climate change; poverty; and access to health care. We all are responsible, and together we can overcome the complex challenges. But here is the main question: how can we help? Well, if we would like to see external changes, the first step we must take is to change ourselves from within. This is a formula that has been given by the Almighty God to mankind, as the following scriptures illustrate:

> ... Indeed, Allah will not change the condition of a people until they change what is in themselves ... (Ar-Raad 13:11)

> Do not conform to the pattern of this world but be transformed by the renewing of your mind ... (Romans 12:2)

We need to refuse to be victims of our traditions and circumstances. By raising our level of consciousness, we can transcend most of our problems with a higher awareness. Each of us can make a positive impact on our world by simply practicing being an authentic human being.

Being an authentic human means being an empathetic person who feels the pain of others and understands their perspectives. Being an authentic person means acknowledging that no one person is better than another and that we all are honored and equal in dignity and rights. In fact, nobody has the right to interfere with others' rights associated with dignity. All humans are equally created by the Almighty God, and we all share equally in the common parentage of the prophet Adam (peace be upon him). Certainly we all are equally blessed and honored by God, as described in the following scriptures:

> And We have certainly honored the children of Adam and carried them on the land and sea and provided for them of the good things and preferred them over much of what We have created, with [definite] preference. (Al-Isra 17:70)

> This is the written account of Adam's family line. When God created mankind, He made them in the likeness of God. He created them male and female and blessed them. And He named them "Mankind" when they were created. (Genesis 5:1–2)

Being an authentic human being means loving others regardless of their cultures, religions, backgrounds, and ethnicities. We should never forget that we all are sharing the same space, the space of mercy and compassion, which has been designed by the Almighty God. Why do we not all help each other for the sake of spreading love in our space? Did we not all come from one source? Is God not the source of love?

> And He is the Forgiving, the Affectionate. (Al-Buruj 85:14)

> Whoever does not love does not know God, because God is love. (1 John 4:8)

Sending love to others simply means understanding, respecting, and accepting others. The importance of love in our relationships is just like the importance of water in our physical bodies. In the same way our bodies get weaker and eventually die if we stop drinking water, our relationships will weaken and eventually die if we stop respecting and accepting each other. Sending love to others does not mean that we should expect something in return. The moment we expect anything in return, we open the door to disappointment and betrayal, and that is not what love is. While it is easy for us to love the people who are nice and respectful to us, it is really a challenge to love the ones who are difficult to love. "If you love those who love you, what credit is that to you? Even sinners love those who love them" (Luke 6:32). Loving difficult people is a challenge and requires some skills. Perhaps we can think of treating others the way we would like them to treat us. "Do to others as you would have them do to you" (Luke 6:31). We truly do not have to physically go and talk to those who persecute us to express our love. Perhaps we can simply pray for them. "But I tell you, love your enemies and pray for those who persecute you" (Matthew 5:44). Maybe the person who is bringing pain and grief to your life is facing some challenges in his or hers, or maybe that person was hurt by someone else in the past. Bestowing mercy on the people who wronged us is a powerful approach that can lead us and others to reach a state of serenity. The more we humble and ground ourselves, the more we can shift the quality of our relationships and attitudes toward others.

Mother Nature is a powerful teacher who provides unconditional love to all creatures without discrimination. Let us learn the meaning of love from a flower, which shares its fragrance to others without discriminating between a white man and a black man. Let us learn how to love others from the sun, which shares its sunlight with all of us without even asking anything in return. Let us learn how to love from Mother Earth, who allows all creatures to walk on her surface without any expectations from anyone. That is what real love looks like.

Nowadays, with all the stressful and complex news we face, we all need to pray together for peace and love. Together, let us ask God to fill our hearts with tranquility, humility, and compassion. Let us ask Him to use each one of us as an instrument of light, peace, and love to others. Today, let us decide to shift our thinking and actions toward unity, healing, and reconciliation. By sharing our prayers, we have an opportunity to connect with others through God. "The Prayer of Saint Francis" is a well-known Christian prayer for peace, also known as "Peace Prayer" or "Make Me an Instrument of Your Peace," by the Italian Saint Francis of Assisi. Let us meditate on this beautiful prayer that is meant to be read by anyone. Are not we all searching for peace?

PRAYER OF SAINT FRANCIS

Lord, make me an instrument of your peace,
Where there is hatred, let me sow love;
Where there is injury, pardon;
Where there is doubt, faith;
Where there is despair, hope;
Where there is darkness, light;
Where there is sadness, joy.
O Divine Master,
Grant that I may not so much seek
To be consoled as to console;
To be understood as to understand;
To be loved as to love.
For it is in giving that we receive;
It is in pardoning that we are pardoned;
And it is in dying that we are born to eternal life.

CHAPTER 22

Are You Listening?

There is no one like you, and there will be no one like you. None of us are perfect, but without you, something will be missing. We need you the way you are because there is nobody in the world who can offer what you can give to the universe.

- I am talking to a father, who can never be replaced. Your family needs your time, support, and love. No one in the world can offer your family what you can.
- I am talking to a mother. Nothing in the world can replace your unconditional love and care for your family. Your mercy and compassion are the greatest blessings to your family.
- I am talking to a brother, the best male friend to his siblings. Your sisters look at you as a defender and a protector. Make sure not to forget that.
- I am talking to a sister, the first female friend to her siblings. You are the best listener and the loyal advisor to your siblings.
- I am talking to a beautiful daughter, the blossoming flower in the house. Your parents look at you as the angel of the house. Your parents are the only people in the world who would give their lives for you. Make sure to take care of them.
- I am talking to a son. Your parents look at you as a man. Make sure to make them proud of you.

Whoever you are, I am talking to you. Your family needs you, and we all need you. Always remember that there is no one like you, and there will be no one like you.

- I am talking to a pastor and imam. You are our spiritual, religious, and social leaders. With your education and spiritual inspiration, we will be guided to the right spiritual path and understand the words of God. We are so thankful to have you in our communities.
- I am talking to a teacher. We need your education, passion, compassion, understanding, and patience. Thanks for being the one who is shaping our future generations.
- I am talking to a janitor. Without you, we would be working in a dirty environment. Thanks for helping us stay healthy and comfortable.
- I am talking to a farmer. We are so appreciative of your hard work. Without you, we would not have the grains, fruits, vegetables, and many other products in our houses.
- I am talking to a medical doctor. Without your knowledge, skills, passion, and experience, we would not have any treatments for our illnesses and injuries. Thank you for taking care of our health.
- I am talking to an engineer. Without you, we would not have cars, airplanes, phones, televisions, and so forth. Thanks for helping us improve our quality of life.
- I am talking to a lawyer. You are the one who defends the accused and advocates for the wronged. Thanks for seeking justice for the victims.
- I am talking to a baker. We are so indebted to have you as one of us. Without you, we would not have bread and pastries in our houses, restaurants, grocery stores, and so on.
- I am talking to a tailor. We are so grateful for your hard work and your creativity. Without you, we would not have our best dresses for all kinds of occasions. Thanks for making us look graceful.

Whoever you are and whatever you do, I am talking to you. You have shown up here for a reason. There is a greatness inside of you. You are worthy. Please do not forget that. Your family, community, and the entire universe need you. Indeed, we all need each other, for we all are connected!

CHAPTER 23

To My Sister in Humanity

I am addressing this chapter to all my sisters in humanity who are going through hardships and pain in this life. Generally speaking, women tend to be more emotional, sensitive, and expressive than men. Unfortunately, we cannot understand the struggles of others until we go through the same difficulties. God has taught me to never let my heart be attached to anything or anyone in this life. God loves us too much to let us be enslaved by this world. Whenever I got attached to anything or anyone, our merciful God took it or him or her away from me to protect me. My first reaction was just like that of a little child who just wants to play with a snake, which has a tender and soft skin, without knowing that the same snake could kill them at any time. I did not learn the lesson the first time, so He allowed me to go through similar experiences multiple times until I learned the lesson and finally got it right.

I would like to share the following letter from my heart straight to my sisters' hearts. In this letter, I share some thoughts that have been helping me move forward in my own life after facing many challenges and adversities. I ask God to use these words of encouragement as a vessel of comfort and solace to uplift and strengthen you, hoping that they can bring you hope and refresh your spirits.

My dear sister,

Peace be upon you.

At first, I would like to remind you that you are enough, worthy, amazing, and have a beautiful soul. God created you and designed you for a specific purpose. You are never alone. Wherever you go, always remember that God is always with you.

There is nothing wrong with you. Yes, maybe life was tough on you and it put you on a path that you do not like, and perhaps that is unfair. Whatever you went through was hard, yet you are still doing your best to face those challenges. I feel the pain and the struggle you are facing today. You had pure and sincere intentions, and yet others misunderstood you, and you got hurt again and again. I want you to know that God is always with you. He heard your voice and every single prayer that came from your sincere heart. He saw your tears; He cares for you and values your sorrow. Always remember that God will never leave you alone.

Whatever you are facing today, always remember Joseph. Recall how his brothers were jealous of him and how they tried their best to put him down by throwing him into the pit. Nevertheless, God lifted him up from being a slave and prisoner to being a leader in Egypt. Never forget how God used all the unfair events that Joseph faced and turned them into something good. We are serving the same God; do you think He will leave you alone?

Whatever you are facing today, always remember the strong faith of Moses's mother. Recall how Pharaoh had a plan to kill all the newborn babies but God had a different plan. God wanted baby Moses to be raised in Pharaoh's house. And yet our merciful God did not ignore the feeling of Moses's mother. As a reward for her unshakeable faith, God not only allowed her to raise her own child through his nursing years but also arranged for her to be paid to nurse him. Well, the same God who took care of that faithful mother will also take care of you and will mend your broken heart. Be still, trust your merciful God, and know that He is the one who directs your steps.

Whatever you are going through today, I want you to know that our merciful God is currently taking care of you, even if you do not see it. He is processing and refining you. He is just preparing you for a breakthrough. Just be patient and never lose hope. Keep your faith strong and trust His plans. He has something great in store for you. Tomorrow you will look back at all you have been through, and you will recognize how God always has the best plan for you. I would like to remind you of God's words:

… But they plan, And Allah plans. And Allah is the best of planners. (Al Anfal 8:30)

"For I know the plans I have for you," declares the Lord, "plans to prosper you and not to harm you, plans to give you hope and a future." (Jeremiah 29:11)

Finally, I would like to remind you that you are serving the Creator of the whole universe. Keep your beautiful smile on your face. Do not be scared of anyone or anything in this life. God is the one who is in control of everything and everyone. He is closer to you than your jugular vein. Always talk to Him and share with Him all your needs and desires. He is the most merciful and the most compassionate.

God bless you,
Your sister in humanity

CHAPTER 24

Light Up Your Candle

You are born with a bright candle to ignite—
A gift from God forever to shine your light.
With all you that you may encounter, share your light.
Let your smile forever shine each day and night,
For you are meant to be a beacon of light.

From envy stay away, or it can harm you.
Revenge never seek, and forgive always do,
For whatever you do will come back to you.
Do not be discouraged for just being you,
For the almighty God will always be with you.

You may be afraid to shine again today,
For you may have been burned by them yesterday.
Whatever you face, keep your faith anyway.
With each passing day, restore your hope and pray,
For the righteous one will show up and stay.

Let us raise our candles and pray to be heard:
A candle of love so joy may be revered,
A candle of peace so hatred can be seared,
A candle of healing so the sick are served,
A candle of hope so faith can't be disturbed.

EPILOGUE

If you are looking for the strongest, God is available.
If you are looking for the best friend, God is available.
If you are looking for the best healer, God is available.
If you are looking for the purest love, God is available.
If you are looking for the best doctor, God is available.
If you are looking for the best listener, God is available.
If you are looking for the best provider, God is available.
If you are looking for the most powerful, God is available.
If you are looking for the best companion, God is available.

We are never alone! God is always available. He is the perfect designer who created everything for a specific purpose. Each one of us is unique and has a purpose to fulfill. Through the connection with God, we can understand ourselves and our real purpose in this journey called life, which in turn can put us on the right path that brings inner peace, fulfillment, and satisfaction into our lives. Because everything happens for a reason, we should never forget that all the challenges and the pain we have been facing are designed to build our characters and help us grow spiritually. Therefore, let us put our full dependence in God and trust His plans.

For every action there is a reaction. This is a universal law: the law of cause and effect. Hence, every tiny action we take will create a ripple effect. So we must be aware and accountable for our own thoughts, emotions, words, and actions. We should never forget that we all have the power to choose our attitudes. So let us make sure to pick the good ones.

Most of us are looking for a better life full of peace and joy and away from anxiety, depression, and stress. However, we cannot change our external experiences until we grow internally. In fact, there are only two choices to consider. The first choice is to accept where we are, blaming others for our mistakes and complaining about everything. The second choice is to decide to walk toward the path of self improvement by practicing the self-awareness of our own self-talk, weaknesses, and actions. Then we must invest in ourselves by taking full ownership of our lives. Indeed, this is not an overnight job, and lots of challenges will be facing us. Seeking God's help, guidance, patience, and strength will indeed help us remain focused, strong, and confident in the face of difficulties.

We may come from different backgrounds and countries, follow different religions, and speak different languages. Nevertheless, we all are spiritual beings that came from and will return to the same source. We all seek to be appreciated and treated with kindness. As humans, we are constantly looking for peace and happiness. Hence, let us start understanding, respecting, and accepting each other so we can grow together despite our differences. Let us be the peacemakers on our planet!

If you are reading my words now, whoever you are, I would like to send you my love and respect. I ask God to protect you and guide you to the right path—the path of spiritual growth. I would also like to thank you for reading this book. I hope you enjoyed it and found it valuable. If you found something to be beneficial while reading, do not forget to share it with your loved ones. Let us spread kindness all together, for we all are connected!

God bless you!

ABOUT THE AUTHOR

Khadije Bazzi was born in Lebanon and raised in Beirut. She received her bachelor's degree in physics from the Lebanese University in 2006. Just after her graduation, she immigrated to the United States and settled in Michigan to continue her journey.

Khadije earned her PhD in physics from Wayne State University in May 2014. The dissertation comprised a study of $LiFePO_4$ as a cathode material for lithium-ion batteries. The dissertation work investigated methods to improve the electrochemical performance of $LiFePO_4$. She published five research papers during her PhD course of study. After her graduate studies, she worked as a fixed-term faculty for two and a half years at Central Michigan University, where she gained valuable experience leading graduate and undergraduate physics lectures for both science and nonscience majors. She joined A123 Systems Automotive Lithium-Ion Solutions in January 2018. She worked as a research scientist for the powder development team for another two and a half years. Currently she is a cell system engineer at General Motors and an adjunct faculty at CMU.

As a Lebanese American Muslim, Khadije strongly believes that we all are connected and that it is our responsibility to understand and respect each other. Hence, she decided to spread her messages to all her brothers and sisters in humanity with the intention of taking one small step toward our unity, healing, and reconciliation.

Printed in the United States
by Baker & Taylor Publisher Services